I SEE YOU

A JOURNEY OUT OF ABUSE BY CREATING A CONVERSATION WITH YOUR INNER CHILD

BRIGIT STRYDER

BALBOA.PRESS
A DIVISION OF HAY HOUSE

Copyright © 2020 Brigit Stryder.

All rights reserved. No part of this book may be used or reproduced by any means, graphic, electronic, or mechanical, including photocopying, recording, taping or by any information storage retrieval system without the written permission of the author except in the case of brief quotations embodied in critical articles and reviews.

Balboa Press books may be ordered through booksellers or by contacting:

Balboa Press
A Division of Hay House
1663 Liberty Drive
Bloomington, IN 47403
www.balboapress.com
844-682-1282

Because of the dynamic nature of the Internet, any web addresses or links contained in this book may have changed since publication and may no longer be valid. The views expressed in this work are solely those of the author and do not necessarily reflect the views of the publisher, and the publisher hereby disclaims any responsibility for them.

The author of this book does not dispense medical advice or prescribe the use of any technique as a form of treatment for physical, emotional, or medical problems without the advice of a physician, either directly or indirectly. The intent of the author is only to offer information of a general nature to help you in your quest for emotional and spiritual well-being. In the event you use any of the information in this book for yourself, which is your constitutional right, the author and the publisher assume no responsibility for your actions.

Cover Art Credit: Lina Baade

Print information available on the last page.

ISBN: 978-1-9822-5756-9 (sc)
ISBN: 978-1-9822-5758-3 (hc)
ISBN: 978-1-9822-5757-6 (e)

Library of Congress Control Number: 2020921314

Balboa Press rev. date: 12/14/2020

DEDICATION

I WOULD LIKE to thank and acknowledge my clients, who have trusted me to be in conversation with their inner child. I want to thank my sons for their unconditional love which has healed and given great company to my inner child in play and companionship. Thank you to my beautiful friends who have walked with me in all my stories and held my hand as I wrote my book. A special thank you to JM.

The wound is the place where the light enters you.

—Rumi

CONTENTS

Dedication v

Introduction xi

Chapter 1	Dear Aria 1
Chapter 2	Sexual Abuse 9
Chapter 3	The Tattoos of Shame 19
Chapter 4	The Ugly Truth 33
Chapter 5	I Am Worth My Next Breath 39
Chapter 6	Beyond the Victim 55
Chapter 7	My Body, My Love 67
Chapter 8	Toxic Loyalty 81
Chapter 9	The Mother Who Won't Stand 95
Chapter 10	Addiction 107
Chapter 11	Match Stick Girl 139
Chapter 12	Leaving My Father's Lap 159
Chapter 13	Patriarchal Soil 179
Chapter 14	The "F" Word 199

Epilogue 225

INTRODUCTION

ALLOW ME TO invite you on a very personal journey out of abuse and into a place of healing. This is a story of scars, scars that have accumulated over multiple generations, leading up to the conditions that would allow abuse and abandonment to touch my own life. To this end, this book is a testimony, a blueprint, a common cause to end the misery of abuse and rise above all the animus and shame it creates.

What I hope to show you, dear reader, is a new beginning, one in which we can all join together in an exodus from our pasts and the feelings of powerlessness that have trapped us both as adults and as children.

Please understand that reading my story could potentially break open painful buried emotions. But know that it has been a true labor of love—love of you, the reader, and of myself, the author. It is a story of hope that seeks to take you to a place beyond the old wounds, back to a place we all deserve to return to.

I make no apology for the candid nature in which I have presented ideas and information in this book since I believe it is the most effective way for you to understand and empathize with the common grief we share as survivors of abuse.

Throughout my career as a psychotherapist, I have investigated an array of mental health and well-being techniques. This exploration has led me to conclude that there is a need for a more in-depth conversation in terms of sexual abuse in all its violations.

I would like to pay homage to the works of John Bradshaw, whose wise and eloquent methodology in relation to our inner child has personally led me out of my feelings of shame and powerlessness, as well as informed the direction and focus of this book.

Statistics indicate that sexual abuse is more likely to occur with a relative or close family friend, and often the child is silenced in order to protect the abuser. As children, we do not always have the emotional language to express our needs, name our boundaries, and address our trauma.

By using the *emotional freedom technique* (EFT), I provide personalized, instructional scripts that will allow you to express your own unspoken thoughts and feelings from the past. Some of you may not be familiar with EFT, I therefore have the great privilege to introduce you to this very precious resource.

Research has shown that brain cells can be altered, even in adulthood, thus increasing the neuroplasticity of the brain. EFT assists with this process by optimizing the connection with neural pathways and psychological learning, as well as synaptic responses.

The founder of EFT, psychologist Dr. Roger Callahan, was able to link stress reduction to tapping gently on particular meridian points located on the body. First identified by the ancient Chinese, these points correspond largely with known acupuncture points and are linked to the amygdala in the brain.

If the amygdala receives perceptual information related to an external threat or danger, it will activate parts of the brain so that we experience increased heart rate and muscle tension, automating us to take action without any conscious thought.

For some of us, the supposed safety of our family home has been more akin to the wilds of the jungle, so we organically respond by pouring a cascade of hormones into our system.

Some of us fight, some of us run away, and some of us emotionally shutdown. Yet very few of these responses truly address our abuse or the trauma we experience, certainly not in a positive way. In fact, these responses are more than likely to reduce our ability to thrive and function effectively, so even after the actual threat is long gone, the hypervigilance generated can last for a lifetime if not addressed properly.

In the end, our bodies become like lightning rods to tension, always anticipating where the next source of abuse and abandonment will emanate from. In this sense, we begin to live our lives in a fearful state, always looking through the jaded lenses of the past.

By tapping on these Meridian points, you are sending a signal to your amygdala to deactivate the fight-flight-freeze response, thereby allowing you to stay calm as you recall stressful memories of past abuse. In this way, you will feel more empowered to look at any psychological challenges with fresh eyes and fresh hope.

Prior to commencing the following EFT tapping process, I strongly recommend that you view the video downloads on my website:

brigitstryder.com.au

EFT
TAPPING POINTS

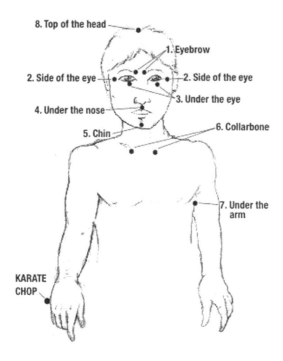

EFT TAPPING POINTS

The KC (karate chop) point is on the outside of your hand closest to your body.

1. eyebrow (EB)
2. side of the eye (SE)
3. under the eye (UE)
4. under the nose (UN)
5. chin (CH)
6. collarbone (CB)
7. under the arm (UA)
8. top of the head (TH)

The first tapping point in the EFT cycle is the "karate chop" point, which is located on the outside of your hand closest to your body. We begin tapping on this point using the setup statement to target our negative feelings, thoughts, and actions.

EFT Setup Statements

In the preceding sentence, include one negative feeling, thought, or action that has occurred for you in the present or past.

Beginning with, speaking out loud, "Even though I feel …" include your own thoughts, feelings, or actions…

For example,

"Even though I am angry [feeling] that I was touched sexually [action] as a child at home by my uncle, I am dirty [thought] because of what my uncle did to me …"

Always end with the following: "I deeply and completely love and accept myself."

Repeat your statements three times as you tap on this point.

You then begin tapping on the other points identified in the "EFT Tapping Points" diagram, starting with the eyebrow (EB) and working your way through to the top of the head (TH).

For example,

EB	I am angry with my uncle.
SE	I feel violated.
UE	I feel dirty.
UN	I feel betrayed.
CH	I felt unsupported.

CB	I was left feeling helpless.
UA	I honor these past and present feelings.
TH	It is safe for me to express myself now

To assist you with tapping, I do provide several rounds of suggested scripts as we explore a range of issues and feelings in the chapters ahead.

While you are tapping, it is recommended that you rate the intensity of your feelings from zero to ten. This will enable you to get a relative sense of the emotional intensity before and after tapping. Ultimately, the goal is to diffuse or pacify the emotion so that it registers as close as possible to a zero.

For example, if I stay in the memory of being yelled at, my fear or hurt is a nine out of ten. I know to keep tapping until I feel myself calm down to a zero. So, when I next think on the memory, I don't have such an intense emotional reaction anymore.

Consider that what you are doing is like a great quest, one that will uncover hidden truths, some of which will be painful yet ultimately liberating. It never ceases to amaze me how solutions to life's challenges naturally arise while practicing EFT, where only powerlessness and sorrow once prevailed.

Another important aspect of this book is the daily rituals I provide at the end of each chapter. These solemn ceremonies allow you to honor the inner child and take back your responsibility for them.

By combining this ritual with the EFT tools provided (beginning in chapter 2), you will have the means to return to your authentic self and give rise to your own untold story, just as I did over a decade ago.

From the outset, I also suggest that you consider getting support from a counselor, trusted friend, or family member, as there is perhaps much buried and untold within, ready to resurface. Reflect deeply upon this, as this is an essential part of your way back to yourself and taking control of your life.

Let us begin this healing together, dear reader. In this, you will no longer be alone.

Brigit Stryder
August 2020

CHAPTER 1
DEAR ARIA

ONE DAY IN early February 2008, I sat in a café feeling emotionally drained and lost. All of me, in that single moment, had reached some kind of spiritual full stop. It was as if I could no longer go forward with this so-called normal way of life. Something had broken loose inside of me, and it was now crying out for change.

Without thinking I picked up a pen and simply began to draw. A child's face appeared and then some hollowed-out eyes, followed by a pair of frail, skinny arms reaching out for a cuddle. As my therapist mind engaged with the image, I immediately recognized I was looking at myself, my own inner child—a seminal sense of being, long lost and forgotten from childhood.

"I see you," I whispered to myself.

It wasn't until March of the same year that I would again look at the picture with a friend. Interestingly, she asked if my inner child had a name. I thought this was a little odd, but then I began to seriously think about her question. Little Brigit was the obvious answer, yet something inside of me spoke the name "Aria." I was to find out later that, in Hebrew, Aria means "lioness-courage"—something that I needed to grow for my inner child and myself.

My friend then asked, "What does she need?"

I pondered this question for a moment and then answered, "Food, Aria needs food."

From that day on, I began placing an offering of milk and a biscuit at the foot of my favorite tree for Aria while saying the words, "I see you, I see you, I see you."

Over time, this frozen aspect of myself began to thaw out. Like a frightened child, she began to take her first timid steps out of the shadows of childhood past into the light.

As I consolidated this new relationship with myself, I reached a kind of existential threshold, whereby I knew my real life would inextricably begin to collide with this new way of being, the way I truly wanted to be.

The first point of impact was my unhappy marriage. At the time of the realization about my inner child, I happened to be reading Elizabeth Gilbert's, *Eat Pray Love*.

I recognized almost immediately that I shared this woman's deep sense of unhappiness, trapped in a relationship in which she was unable to voice her pain and fears to her husband. The words in her book, "Tell the truth, tell the truth, tell the truth," would continuously resonate in my mind.

It was a punch to my chest, as I had come to realize I was held hostage in a living lie. The essential truth was that I was struggling to love my husband, by telling myself I must be with this man because I married him. Moreover, he could not see who I was becoming; he could not see me.

But who was *I*? Who was I becoming?

There were some loving periods in my marriage; however, it was offset by my husband's emotional abuse, alcoholism, and abandonment. My sense of self corroded over time as a wife, as a mother, and as a woman. The early months of ritual with my inner child were to eventually equip me with the perseverance to navigate my way through these difficult times.

Finally, I embraced the realization that I did not want to be with my husband anymore. I neither had the inclination nor the will to carry on with what had become the artifice of a loving relationship. To this end, I surrendered, as I could not see how I would keep this part of my life and preserve the whole. It was then I decided to leave my marriage of thirteen years.

Even though the aftermath of the breakup was horrendous, a healthy boundary had emerged, one in which my adult self took the wounded inner child's hand and stood up for her. This transformation did not happen overnight. Instead, it grew gradually like a muscle gained from daily exercise in a gym.

I have now lit my candle and fed my inner child, without fail, for the past fourteen years. Subsequently, an inner strength has not only arisen but is now well and truly consolidated within me. My prayer, my daily mantra of, "I see you," and "You matter to me," lifted me out of the ashes of my own self-abasement into a place of spiritual nourishment, a safe harbor of the soul.

If you are interested in a similar ritual for your inner child, there are many variations to how you may want to undertake this. For me, it was establishing an altar in my home where I could place my thimble of milk and a biscuit, which I replenish every day. I also have a photo of myself as a young girl when the abuse took place, so she is literally seen. In addition to this, I have crystals and small figurines of the feminine standing with Aria.

Exercise

Set up your own altar to your inner child. The kinds of objects and things you may want to include could be

- *photos of yourself, places, or people that are dear to you*
- *flowers, stones, shells, or any other natural objects*
- *toys, ornaments, or other man-made things that may have sentimental value*

- *images or other representations of deities that have particular spiritual significance to you*
- *inspirational poems, affirmations, or quotes*

Basically, you are looking for things that will educate, empower, and inspire you and your inner child within.

Will you make a daily offering of sorts to your inner child (e.g., leaving food or objects, lighting candles, burning oils, and so on)?

Where will you place the altar? Will it be kept in a private sanctuary or in a public place for the world to see?

Write a prayer or affirmation to honor your own inner child. The task is to see the child within, whatever way you choose.

Does your inner child have a name? If so, does it have some special meaning or significance to you?

It may seem weird or even challenging to some that a relationship to the inner child is required. But in many ways, it does not differ entirely from commonplace practices adopted in psychoanalysis, whereby the strategies used to deal with dysfunctional personality traits can often be traced back to our early childhood experiences, which include abuse and abandonment.

An intrinsic part of finding or re-establishing this relationship with our inner child is to ask ourselves questions like the following: Who am I really? Where is that joy I once knew? Am I really in charge of myself if I cannot find what truly makes me happy? Am I making choices based upon the pain and abandonment I suffered in the past? When exactly did I lose my inner child? What event(s) occurred to erode, block, or make me forget this part of myself?

In the end, how you nourish your own inner child is up to you. But doing so is necessary in order to establish a strong basis upon which you can challenge and address the abuse you have encountered in your life.

In rediscovering my own inner child, I have found it useful to have an open conversation about my sexual abuse, which first disconnected me from Aria (inner child). A useful inroad into this was to write a letter to her.

The following is an example.

A Letter to Aria (Four Years Old)

Dear Aria,

You are brave and beautiful. I see you!

I see you through compassionate eyes, hurt by someone you trusted and loved. I am sorry your parents did not see your trauma. I am sorry that you were not protected. I am sorry you were violated in ways that hurt you so much.

I understand you chose not to remember and to shut away the pain for so long. And that's okay, Aria. I validate you. I honor you. I know your nightmares were your way of dealing with the memories.

Here me now, Aria—hear me loud. The actions of your abusers were never your fault! Never, never, never! Nothing you did as a four-year-old could invite abuse.

You are a sweet, innocent child; you always have been. You have an amazing spark that keeps your loving heart beating, despite all the guilt that you have carried.

Just remember, I love you, and I will stand by you now. You are a child finding your way back to your authentic self. We will heal together. We will learn to live again with happiness and joy.

I am so very proud of you. I am you. I am what you hoped I would become. For that, I am thankful.

> *I am the mother of three magnificent sons, with the heart of a lioness. You beat with my heart. You have helped me keep them safe.*
>
> *Enjoy this world and all its gifts. You are free now, my love, to go ride, laugh, and sing.*
>
> *I love you,*
>
> *Brigit*

Exercise

Consider writing your own letter to your inner child. In completing this process, you may want to write several letters to address one or more specific event(s), in relation to abuse and abandonment.

So many of us in this world are emotionally and spiritually hungry. We act upon this impulse, often irrationally, like babies seeking out basic nourishment from our mothers or significant loved ones. This is perhaps why so many of us turn to addiction and other unhealthy preoccupations, in order to feed these undernourished or broken aspects of ourselves.

For this reason, the symbolic feeding of my own inner child with milk and cookies is important to address this imbalance. Thus, we create the necessary steps toward addressing our inner spiritual deprivation.

Despite all of my professional training and therapeutic processes, this simple childlike ritual of affirming my inner child has been instrumental in regaining what had been broken and displaced.

Day after day, year after year, I've seen my inner child becoming less invisible and more central to my core values and beliefs in my everyday life. Just like a child growing in my womb, I have become my own spiritual mother. In this, I learned to love her and myself as it should have always been.

An afterglow of joy has emerged in me. And though my immediate life circumstances are still changing, I know I have sown the seeds for my own internal revolution, a birthing of my authenticity from my heart and from my soul.

Finally, I want to name my deep gratitude to the beautiful Zora Neale Hurston. Her words, 'there is no agony like bearing an untold story inside you', unzipped my heart and led me to write this book, so I may help others release their unheard agonies that have been silent for too long. Ironically not just silent from others, but from self to self.

Know that as we enter the chapters ahead, I am holding your hand as you begin to meet your inner child. Be patient and kind to her/him as they share the stories and conversations that have remained buried.

Ritual

Light a candle to your inner child and say,

I see you.

I love you.

Thank you for your bravery.

Thank you for your story.

I am listening.

Chapter 2
Sexual Abuse

I WAS SEXUALLY abused as a child.

Once when I was four years old and on repeated occasions after turning twelve. This resulted in anxiety and bedwetting. I also developed a disorder known as trichotillomania, whereby I had an irresistible urge to pull out my own eyelashes, creating moments of relief and pleasure. I suffered these symptoms until my early teens. However, I did not recognize it was the result of my sexual abuse until my early fifties.

Back when I was a child, therapy was not the *done thing*, especially in a working-class suburb. I did go to the hospital as a child for medical tests for my excessive urination. However, no one directly asked me about my feelings or recognized that I was suffering from a post-traumatic stress disorder. The subsequent shame I endured as a young girl, disfigured with no eyelashes, continues to affect me to this day.

As a young teenager, I was frequently and inappropriately touched by my father while he was drunk. Having already experienced sexual abuse at four, my body's response was to go into a freeze mode. As a result, I never yelled at him or tried to get away.

Subsequently, my sense of self-love was virtually annihilated. Later, I would learn to intellectually process what had been done to me. However, back then, I was a little girl forced to carry the shame alone, knowing full well that the abuse would happen time and time again.

As mentioned in the first chapter, I have reclaimed my inner child for fourteen years now. This journey back into myself has given me the tools to step off the trauma treadmill and bring my girl home. It was as if I had pushed the stage writer off the chair and begun to type a new script for my life. Once there was an abused child who was invisible, but now she is seen!

Regrettably, many sexual abuse victims never get the opportunity to resolve their experiences. They remain silent for fear of repercussions or simply don't know how to articulate what has happened to them. Thus the trauma continues on in their mind, body, and spirit, and they never receive the correct nourishment and healing. This could well describe my situation six years ago. Until I had a dream…

I am in my home. I have guests arriving for a party. I become alarmed when I discover that the front porch light isn't working.

I think to myself, "How can my friends see the front door in the dark?"

I get my uncle to fix the light. He is the father of the cousin who abused me when I was four years old. He is grumpy about doing it, but he does it anyway.

Next thing I know, the toilet begins to block up, and I panic. "It needs to work for my guests!"

The toilet is positioned in the kitchen (the symbolic place of alchemical and transformational change), and I have to fix it myself.

I feel physically sick as I work my way through the human waste, down into the toilet shaft. In the dream, my hand penetrates deep into the earth and pulls out the sword of Excalibur, representing truth and integrity. I swing the sword in the room, and in one clean slice, I cut off my uncle's head. I am calm, and I feel a renewed sense of confidence tingle through my body…

Reflecting upon the dream, I believe my uncle was a representation of my father. My hand moving through the human waste symbolized for me the blockages of abandonment and self-loathing I was still experiencing in my life.

This dream propelled me into action. Almost immediately, I knew my past abuse had to be addressed, and this could only be done by directly challenging my father after decades of silence.

I drove to my family home, calmly sat down with my parents, and spoke about my feelings of shame and violation in respect to my father's actions. Remarkably, he cried and apologized, yet he claimed that he had no memory of the actual abuse.

Despite my father's inability to recall these events, it was still a time of healing for me. I knew my daily attendance to the inner child ritual had generated the capacity to address my father's abuse, creating the emotional foundation that enabled me to face my ancient fears.

As I reflect on this part of my story, I am still discovering how much was unseen and unheard by my parents, especially my mother. (I will discuss this in a later chapter.) I remember that despite how far I had traveled, I still wanted someone, anyone, to take away the pain. Like a child, I needed others to assume all the responsibility for what had happened to me. However, in the end, I turned the shame inward, robbing me of my childhood happiness and joy.

So often in my practice, I have heard of similar accounts of childhood self-blame, whereby my clients felt they should have made better decisions, reacted with more courage, or put up a better fight against their abuser. The truth is we have done nothing wrong. Yet either in response to the abusers' threats or deceptions, we believe we are somehow culpable for their actions.

Many of these clients have never been invited by their parent or significant others to discuss their feelings. At worst, it is the parent or trusted family member who is responsible for the abuse, leaving the child with the question, "Whom can I tell?"

Potentially, this can digress into an "us or them" mentality, thus having a destructive impact upon the family unit as a whole.

The abuser may consciously or unconsciously set about undermining the credibility of the victim, minimalizing any future repercussions against them. So, in this context, the victim feels the intense added burden of protecting his or her family from the destructive ramifications of exposing the abuser.

So let us go gently, dear reader, and be brave. These old and buried places will resurrect raw, painful memories and perhaps some old, angry ghosts.

As we begin, I want you to feel safe and nourished, knowing I am holding your hand in this process. Please feel free to adapt any of the words in the tapping scripts to your own specific circumstances.

Tapping Script 1

KC   Even though I have been sexually abused, I deeply and completely love and accept myself.

KC   Even though I have old memories of being sexually abused, I deeply and completely love and accept myself.

KC   Even though I wasn't kept safe, I deeply and completely love myself.

EB   I am a victim of sexual abuse.

SE   I have kept silent about this.

UE.   I have just wanted to forget.

UN   I have been afraid to remember.

CH   But now I must speak out.

CB	Though it brings up so much hurt.
UA.	I know it must be done.
TH	I know it must be so.

EB	It is safe for me to remember.
SE	It is safe for me to begin.
UE.	I am safe to share my experiences.
UN	I deserve to be safe now.
CH	I deserve to be cared for.
CB	I am happy to receive all the support I can.
UA	It is time I move forward.
TH	It is time for me to release the old trauma.

EB	I will honor my inner child.
SE	I will honor the innocence within me.
UE	I deserve to be free from this trauma.
UN	I want to heal now.
CH	I want to release all the pain.
CB	I am tired of all the pain.
UA	I am tired of all the secrets.
TH	I am tired of being alone with this.

EB	I release all the terror.
SE	I release all the fear.
UE	From the cells of my body.
UN	It is safe to revisit my past.
CH	I choose to look at my memories.
CB	I will be courageous.
UA	I will be strong.
TH	And I will be free.

EB	It is possible to tell the truth.
SE.	It is possible to heal from sexual abuse.
UE	No one will stop this.
UN	Not even myself.
CH	I am at the beginning.
CB	Just the beginning.
UA	It is within my control.
TH.	It is safe for me to be seen.

Take a moment to just feel what's in your mind and body right now. Keep tapping on each point and receive each word as you speak it.

Exercise

Try to write down your own version of a script, and consider some of the following suggestions while using it:

- *Commit to using the script regularly at different times of the day.*
- *Feel what it is like to say the lines out loud. Words and phrases take on a whole different meaning when read outside of your head.*
- *Savor each line that stands out for you. Repeat it over and over again.*
- *Be honest about what else you may be feeling. There is no point in simply moving through the script if it has no meaning for you.*
- *Don't be afraid to laugh, scream, or cry, in order to release deep-seated emotions from within.*
- *There is no rush. Know how to pace yourself.*
- *Swear like a trooper if that helps!*
- *Remember to drink fluids and rest in between tapping scripts.*

In preparing for the next tapping script, I want you to reflect on how you feel toward your abuser.

What are you feeling?

Where is the emotion in your body?

<u>Tapping Script 2</u>

KC   Even though as a child I felt frightened and hurt by you, _____ [name the person], I love and accept who I am.

KC   Even though it was wrong what _____ [name of person] did to me, I love and accept who I am.

KC Even though I felt afraid to share my story about _____ [name the person], I love and accept who I am.

EB I am angry with you, _____ [name of abuser].

SE I am afraid of you, _____ [name the abuser].

UE I want to express my hurt.

UN I am disgusted by you, _____ [name of the abuser].

CH I feel violated by you.

CB I feel all this tightness in my body.

UA I feel sick.

TH I feel tired.

EB I was only _____ [your age at the time of abuse].

SE I thought I could trust you.

UE You disrespected my body.

UN You violated my boundaries.

CH You caused me so much grief.

CB I will no longer hold on to this trauma.

UA	I'm telling *my* story now!
TH	You're not telling it anymore.

EB	So much broken trust.
SE	So many lies.
UE	I release all the shame you caused me, _____[name the person].
UN	And now it's time for healing.
CH	I am here for my inner child.
CB	I am here for a new beginning.
UA	It's such a relief to get my story in the open.
TH	You can't stop me now.

EB	I was just a child.
SE	I had no way of controlling the situation back then.
UE	I had no way to protect myself.
UN	I commit to healing.
CH	I commit to this tapping process.
CB	I will release this abuse from my body.
UA	I will release this abuse from my mind.
TH	I was a beautiful child.

EB	And I will be beautiful once more.
SE	I deserve inner peace.
UE	I deserve more happiness.
UN	I deserve more love.
CH	This is a new beginning for me.
CB	Blessings on me.
UA	Blessings on the child within.
TH	The silence is over.

Breathe, and breathe again.

Ritual

>Light your candle.
>
>Say to your inner child.
>
>>I am holding you close.
>>
>>As you release the secrets, the terror, the fears.
>>
>>Surrender it all now.
>>
>>Your forced silence is over.
>>
>>Go to sleep now.
>>
>>You are safe in my arms.
>>
>>I love you.

CHAPTER 3
THE TATTOOS OF SHAME

WHEN I HEAR the word *shame*, I feel a dreadful, familiar tightness in the pit of my stomach. It feels like the word has been tattooed into my skin, stained into my soul.

Shame is a painful feeling that rises up when you feel a deep regret or worthlessness. Perhaps you have told yourself, or have been told you are a 'bad' person, who has acted dishonorably and the feeling of being scolded, even labelled responsible is unbearable.

In my case, my four-year old believed that she had acted dishonorably alongside her cousin, and therefore told herself that she shared a responsibility for the sexual abuse. It is sad to admit that I felt the rot of this shame in my heart for decades.

When a child takes on the sins of the abuser, a voice starts to speak to him or her in the form of an inner critic. In my case, this voice became nestled in my own mind like a dark monster, shutting out all the joy and happiness afforded to me as a child. The trauma eventually permeated my unconscious mind, and I started to be convinced that every ugly tattoo of shame was real.

The sad truth of the matter is that these seeds may have been planted in the mind of the perpetrator long before the actual abuse occurred. Thus, a cycle of abuse is tattooed by one abuser onto another, like a baton, passed on from one generation to another.

It is therefore crucial to recognize that the actions of abuse and the subsequent shame incurred does not have to determine the way you live your life. The initial goal then is to simply accept that it is possible to be beautiful again, to be whole again, to be safe again.

Part of this process of healing involves accepting that our hatred and fear of our abuser can be turned inward, keeping us frozen in a perpetual cycle of anger, depression, and silent rage.

In some cases, shame has been reinforced by the values and principles underpinning many of our traditional and religious institutions. Consciously or unconsciously, they have punished or even reinforced shame as a weapon of abuse, to keep the victim silent.

Notably, there is a growing body of scientific evidence suggesting that trauma can be transmitted to our offspring because of epigenetic changes in our DNA. The same reports also indicate that positive, self-affirming techniques, such as EFT, can correct these anomalies. Effectively, we can scrub off our tattoos of shame and overcome our afflictions of abuse.

At this point, it is useful to remember that EFT stands for emotional freedom technique—freedom from our toxic relationships, freedom from our faulty thinking, and ultimately freedom from our inner critic.

Understandably, certain words or phrases may give rise to a powerful sense of shame. However, these thoughts and feelings are not actually put inside of us, as such. As simple as this may sound, it is important to acknowledge, since this is the key to overcoming given emotional states of mind. It is us, in our minds, generating these negative impressions.

It then follows that we can reframe, displace, or even eliminate given thoughts or feelings from our consciousness. Believe me, I know firsthand that this is no easy task! But despite the initial sadness, distress, or anger this may bring, it is important to begin this process. For me, I had a vision of these feelings and thoughts etched into my mind and parts of my body. What I refer to as "tattoos of shame."

Exercise

Describe your own "tattoos of shame." What are the words or sentences inked into your skin, into your mind, into your heart?

Here are some examples: I am angry and self-loathing, dislike, fear, shame, hate, victim, rage, I am not worthy, hopelessness, exhausted, stay silent, guilty, punish me, punish them, suffering, alone, isolated, loser, whore, slut, rejected by God, rejected by the world, rejected by my father, rejected by my mother, names (of the people that I blame), I am bad, sadness, confused, fragile, crazy, mad, stupid, powerless, vulnerable, shattered boundary, secrets, unlovable, my fault, unsupported, broken.

Imagine where they would be located on your body?

How have your tattoos shaped your life and relationships to date?

How would you describe your tattoo to your loved ones, to a friend, to your parents, or perhaps to your children?

How would you describe them to your abuser?

Okay, take a deep, cleansing breath. That was hard work!

Now, in your own words, gently acknowledge the thoughts and feelings associated with your tattoos of shame. Stay calm and separate from them; just try to sense that they are present and nothing else.

Close your eyes and imagine a point of bright light. If you are spiritual, the light may be linked to something you consider divine and nurturing. If not, imagine it is part of a healing force within yourself. When you are ready, give over these feelings and thoughts about your "tattoos of shame" to the light and begin the following tapping script.

Tapping Script 3

KC   Even though I feel all this pain and sadness, I deeply and completely love and accept myself.

KC   Even though I have all these tattoos of shame that I am trying to get rid of, I love and accept myself.

KC   Even though I have so many negative feelings and thoughts, I love and forgive myself.

EB   All this shock.

SE   All this trauma.

UE   All these tattoos.

UN   I thought they were a part of me.

CH   I thought they were permanent.

CB   Hateful beliefs like [Insert the tattoos of shame you identified in the previous exercise].

UA   Some I inked in myself.

TH   Some were inked into me.

EB   All of these tattoos.

SE   They don't belong on me anymore.

UE   They never belonged on me.

UN   It is safe for me to remove them now.

CH	Even though they have been there for so long.
CB	It is time to give them to the light.
UA	Let the light take them away.
TH	I will no longer be shamed by them.
EB	Instead [Take a deep breath, dear reader].
SE	I will rejoice!
UE	I will release the pain!
UN	To the light!
CH	To the new dawn!
CB	I will love myself again! I will love my body again!
UA	I have a good heart.
TH	It will be safe again.
EB	I am able to create a new me.
SE	I have begun to see my true beauty.
UE	I welcome new hope.
UN	I am deserving of it.
CH	Where I felt shame, I will feel compassion.
CB	Where I felt blame, I will feel sympathy.

UA   This is the beginning of the end.

TH   I will be free to love. Blessed be!

Now.

Breathe …

Breathe …

Breathe …

Beautiful, beautiful you.

Well done for hanging in there. Rest now, and gather your thoughts and feelings.

Exercise

Can I suggest you now have a shower and imagine washing away your tattoos of shame? See them as flaking scabs ready to fall away from your body with each scrubbing motion. Notice those tattoos that do not fall away so easily. Direct portions of the tapping script just completed toward them. See what effect this might have. Does it weaken them? Does it give rise to other new feelings and thoughts—the tattoos under the tattoos?

One of the emotional scars of sexual abuse is the feeling of not belonging with our family, or even our community. This deeply tribal sense of not fitting in can be the product of our own forced isolation, by which we seek personal protection, or perhaps we are afraid that somehow the tattoos we harbor psychologically will become visible to those we love and those we fear.

From my personal and professional experience, it is not unusual that other immediate or extended family members are being abused and shamed into a forced silence. This can stop you from ever asking a very simple question, "Is this happening to you?"

Since the shame is hidden, it may manifest into withdrawn or aggressive behaviors. Parents or siblings who are unaware of the abuse may simply dismiss the victim's behaviors as weird, sensitive, or eccentric. This may prompt further dysfunction, such as ongoing cycles of ridicule, miscommunication, and conflict. For me, this manifested in a feeling of isolation and not belonging to my family.

For example, my family would constantly joke around and say I was adopted. Seemingly friendly banter would appear to be loaded with all matter and meaning for me, triggering my shame and further feelings of isolation. This found its way into how I formed my personality and attitudes towards life in general.

My tattoos of shame shaped how I interacted not only in my home environment but also while at school. My ability to socialize and entertain friendships was hindered by my fear that they would somehow see the shame I carried. This was further complicated as I would enter this space with missing eyelashes, fresh from yet another night of bedwetting. I felt out of my depth to cope with the stares I received, mixed with my own paranoia that everyone saw me as weird and stupid.

Playtime was the hardest part of my school day. Children would excitedly run out when the bell rang. However, I was socially ill equipped to deal with this activity and spent most of my time in a toilet cubicle. This little space was where I would take refuge and silently feel the depth of my loneliness.

It was not until my late twenties that I would reveal my story to one of my sisters. To my great dismay, she too divulged that she had been sexually abused by our father. Though I was deeply saddened by this disclosure, we were able to form a loving bond that did not exist when we were children. For that, I will be eternally grateful. Thank you, Sis.

Let's do some tapping.

Tapping Script 4

KC   Even though I felt lonely and isolated as a child, I love and accept myself now.

KC   Even though I still feel like I don't belong in the company of my family, I love and accept myself.

KC   Even though remaining withdrawn and isolated has become part of my identity, I know I can change.

EB   All this loneliness.

SE   I feel it deeply.

UE   Sometimes I feel I don't belong.

UN   Sometimes I feel I don't belong to anyone.

CH   It hurts me to feel unattached.

CB   I feel like an emotional orphan.

UA   I feel alone in my story of abuse.

TH   So much has been lost, so much has been broken.

EB	The abuse is over, but the pain remains.
SE	I am safe now.
UE	Safe to express my loneliness.
UN	Safe to share it with those who really care for me.
CH	The child within deserves connection.
CB	The child within deserves to belong.
UA	The child within is safe with me.
TH	The child within will never be alone again.

EB	I am willing to reach out to others.
SE	I am willing to reach for my inner child.
UE	I no longer need to be isolated.
UN	It is safe to reach out for support.
CH	Telling others my story brings me closer to them.
CB	I choose to seek refuge in this.
UA	I no longer have to hide my deep loneliness.
TH	I am free now to share my silent pain.

Repeat the sequence as many times as you need.

Exercise

Many parents keep photos of their children in their wallet. Consider doing the same thing but with a photo of yourself as a young child. Perhaps this is a photo of you prior to or after the abuse. Keep her or him close to you during the day like a caring parent would. You may also have some affirming words written on the back of the photo. This may help lift some of the loneliness or pain you have historically felt.

This section is specifically targeted at those of us whose tattoos of shame can extend into physical wounds, such as sexually transmitted diseases.

In Giorn's research paper, "The Impact of Sexually Transmitted Diseases on the Quality of Life: Application of Three Validated Measures," he states, "Women with STDs experience frustration, anxiety, anger, fear of rejection, isolation, guilt, embarrassment (and) shame." Giorn further comments that these women may, have the feeling of being "dirty" and the fear of negative reactions from others. As a result, [they] experience a lack of social functioning and a low quality of life. Furthermore, such feelings can lead to decreased self-esteem.

Giorn. It. Ost. Gin. Giornale Italiano di Ostetricia e Ginecologia CIC Edizioni Internazionali 2013 November-December; 35(6): 722–727. ISSN: 0391-9013 Published online 2014 March 19.

Concurrently, these negative feelings can also potentially exacerbate psychological scarring linked to past sexual abuse. As a result, the victim may experience further withdrawal from positive intimacy. This can also reawaken our inner critic, taking the form of thinking such as the following:

"It's my fault."

"I didn't use a condom / I failed to protect myself."

"This always happens to me."

"I deserve this."

"I was stupid to trust him or her."

"I feel dirty now."

"How could I allow myself to be in this situation?"

"Who will love me now?"

While we may develop an intense sense of self-loathing, we can also become so enraged by the onset of an STD that we overreact. This may lead to a renewed sense of violation and betrayal, resulting in severe interpersonal conflict or even the breakdown of intimate relationships.

And though you may be inflicted with a given STD, you can still step up and free yourself of the feelings and thoughts associated with your affliction.

Exercise

- Write down what sexual diseases you may have been afflicted with, and whether they were permanent or temporary?
- What was the nature of the symptoms, and how did they affect your life?
- What was the outcome in terms of your relationship with your infected partner?
- Was the STD a result of sexual abuse?

May I suggest, at this point, that you look at Louise Hay's book *You Can Heal Your Life*. In it, she provides a useful guide to combating negative feelings that you may hold toward physical afflictions, such as STDs. By saying her positive affirmations daily, you can create a positive stream of consciousness, promoting personal forgiveness and self-love.

Time for tapping.

Tapping Script 5

KC   Even though I feel 'marked' by this disease, I love and accept myself.

KC   Even though I feel like its return is an attack on my body, I love and accept myself.

KC   Even though I feel deep shame for being infected by my [name the condition], I love and accept myself now.

EB   My [name the condition] reminds me of my painful past.

SE   My [name the condition] reminds me of what I desperately want to forget.

UE   Just another tattoo to scrub off.

UN   Just another thing telling me there's something wrong with me.

UC   My [name the condition].

CB   I don't want it anymore.

UA   I am so sick of it.

TH   I am so sick of all the anger and hurt it has caused.

EB   It is time to move on.

SE   Time to move from the shame.

UE   I give it to the light.

UN   I give it to what is good in me.

UC   Let it become a mark of truth.

CB   Let it remind me I can move on.

UA   I will no longer be held hostage.

TH   I am taking back all of my body, even this disease.

(Place one hand at the source of the disease and continue)

EB   Every inch, every centimeter is mine.

SE   My body is filled with my love.

UE   I have taken it back now.

UN   No disease here.

UC   Love is my guide.

CB   Love is my medicine.

UA   My body is a vessel of strength.

TH   Blessed be my body.

Well done!

As a society we must challenge our tattoos of shame so that our children, and our children's children will learn to acknowledge and speak up against all forms of abuse. Thereby leading to a culture of sympathy and compassion that understands the destructive, negative associations with sexual abuse.

Perhaps, like any plague, we can eradicate or at least contain the ill effects of abuse, abandonment, and shame. Through growing worldwide awareness of its great social cost, we can begin to heal one family, one community, one society at a time until perhaps a day will come when it is a thing of the past, and we are all safe. In this, at least, we can hope.

Ritual

Light a candle.

Say a prayer to your inner child.

> I light this candle to send love.
>
> Dear, dear child.
>
> You are safe.
>
> Come, my love, let me wash away your tears,
>
> Wash away the hurt,
>
> Wash away your shame,
>
> So you are left clean.
>
> Clean in your heart,
>
> Clean in your mind,
>
> Clean in your body.
>
> And then you will thrive.

CHAPTER 4
THE UGLY TRUTH

ENTWINED WITHIN ALL my tattoos of shame was a deep-seated sense of ugliness, making me feel I was unworthy of authentic love. A clear example I previously gave was my trichotillomania, which literally left me looking different to everyone else. The shame and torment associated with this condition was sometimes unbearable. Yet it was the only tool I had at my disposal to fully express my hidden agonies.

Unfortunately, I became frozen developmentally in my abuse, setting me on a trajectory toward unhealthy relationships, that led to a great deal of promiscuity in my early twenties. At first, I perceived this as a badge of honor, the trappings of a liberated woman. But later I discovered that I was actually acting in accordance with the preconditioning inflicted upon me by my abusers.

Like a jigsaw puzzle falling into place, I could see how I allowed men to use me purely for sex. I continuously sought out sex in this fashion to make myself feel special, just as I had felt with my father. Ultimately my need to be perceived as beautiful was unquenchable, eventually backfiring and creating ever-increasing cycles of self-abasement and loss of identity. Eventually, it led me to conclude I was better off staying single, which I did for many years.

In all of this, I simply could not unhinge myself from the idea that my nasty little secret of abuse kept me ugly, inside and out. It was only when I began to consider the very basis upon which real beauty is defined that I realized I needed to reframe my own thinking about it.

Feminine beauty has been largely based upon subjective points of view at given times in history. An example of this is how sexually enticing images of women in nineteenth-century art often depicted beautiful women as shapely and voluptuous, while anorexic, prepubescent girls are now considered to be the height of attractiveness and fashion. We cannot even trust the images we are looking at today as they have been manipulated out of all recognition by computer-generated imaging.

So it is important to consider who exactly is coming up with all this stuff, these "measuring sticks" of human attractiveness and self-worth. It would be easy to simply lay the blame exclusively at the feet of the patriarchy. But women have had their part to play, through their judgments, their words, and, most of all, through their silent compliance. (I will explore this in greater depth later in the book).

In hindsight, my understanding of love did not match the reality. Yet I still failed to see where the true source of beauty had always been, on the inside, within me. This hackneyed truism is the stuff of legends and an endless source of inspiration for internet memes. But how many of us actually embrace it, especially those among us who have been sexually abused? How many terrible relationships and false starts have we endured only to arrive at this undeniable truth?

It really is that simple and that hard. Even on my most confident days, I still suffer from bouts of ugliness. But through EFT therapy and good old common sense, I can now finally attest to at least being on the road to appreciating the rich tapestry of my own life, which makes me truly beautiful in my own eyes and in the eyes of those I love. I know that this is a unique gift of beauty that is mine and mine alone.

So, it is time to shatter the illusion of ugliness. Shine your light into these dark places, and know *you are beautiful*. You always have been. Time to get with that!

Let's tap on the ugly truth about beauty.

Tapping Script 6

KC   Even though I have a deep-seated belief that I am ugly, I profoundly love and accept myself.

KC   Even though when I look in the mirror and see only my imperfections, I love and accept myself.

KC   Even though I've come to believe I am unattractive, I forgive myself for thinking this way.

EB   All this ugliness.

SE   It never was mine.

UE   All of this ugliness.

UN   I give it back to the world.

CH   I will no longer live with it.

CB   Because I am a beautiful person.

UA   Beautiful in my own right.

TH   My face, my body, my soul.

EB   Are all there for me to enjoy.

SE   I am safe to receive the attraction of those who deserve me.

UE   The dark ugliness, the dark lie.

UN   There will only be light here now.

CH   Light on my hidden wound.

CB	Light in my wounded heart.
UA	I will stand tall and beautiful in my body.
TH	There is only beauty here to be found.
EB	I am first.
SE	It stops with me.
UE	I can keep my beautiful self safe now.
UN	No one can ever take it from me again.
CH	I have so much to give.
CB	It will only grow.
UA	I am safe in my own beauty.
TH	I am safe in my own graciousness.

Continue to tap and consider the true meaning of being beautiful. As each ugly sensation emerges, shed light upon it. Do not let it overcome you. Try to remain focused and observe your emotions and feelings as you transform each point of ugliness.

If you still feel stuck and unconvinced by your true beauty, use the following KC tapping point and say over and over, "Even though it is not possible or safe for me to feel beautiful right now, I will learn to love and accept who I am."

If you feel your mind drifting or being overcome by feelings of ugliness, have a short break and then refocus on the preceding tapping statement.

Another important part of this process to finding your inner beauty is to free yourself from the cruel words of the past and the present—those words that burrowed deep into your soul until you could not tell the difference between your truth and their lies, the same words that defined you and made you feel safe but kept you small. Time to let them all go!

Here are a series of words that I have needed to let go: boring, stupid, opinionated, scatterbrained, trouble/bad, fat, angry, frigid, freak, weird, scary, lazy, out there, moody, space cadet, displeasing, horrible, nasty, revolting, gross.

Exercise

What ugly words can you think of that have been directed at yourself—words that are imprinted in your mind, that have influenced you all your life? Now reflect upon their internal logic and point of origin.

Consider the following:

- *Why were they said? In what context?*
- *When did they start?*
- *Who said these words? Why?*
- *Do they still hurt, or do you feel differently toward them?*
- *What purpose did they serve others?*
- *If you heard them said to a child or a similar person to you, how would you react?*
- *Do these words continue to influence you today? Why? How?*
- *Does your existing partner use these words in reference to you and others? What can you do about it if he or she does?*

Okay, time to think beyond the square peg, or even the round peg. Let notions of beauty fit you, and you not fit them. This is not to suggest you undertake some great violent upheaval of the soul but a quiet, slow-moving process that incrementally increases in your everyday life.

To achieve this, we need to commit ourselves to new and inspired ways of seeing the world and our place in it. It is our job, and our job alone, to forge these new links to our inner beauty. It will change the relationships we choose, since we will no longer be acting from a place of undernourishment, jealousy, possessiveness, and other negative self-serving traits. We will learn to welcome this inner beauty so all may flourish.

In closing, let me say you are on a brave quest of the heart. So stand tall and true to yourself, and do not be afraid of the possibilities of real beauty, for by doing so, you may discover the most elusive, the most important and beautiful lover in your life—yourself.

Ritual

Light your candle.

Tell your inner child,

> I see you.

> I see you now.

> From my own heart.

> From my own beauty.

> From my own soul.

> The great journey into love is about to begin.

> Blessings upon real love.

> Blessings upon all things beautiful.

CHAPTER 5
I AM WORTH MY NEXT BREATH

MY FATHER'S APPROACH to running the family household was along traditional lines, whereby his word was law. I often felt powerless and confused under his absolute rule as the "boss." For most of my childhood, I was left feeling vulnerable and silent, wondering if this was the day he would be my protector instead of my abuser.

What is now apparent (and somewhat mortifying to me) was how my identity was so entwined with my sexual abuse. In the course of our childhood, our parents teach us many things: to speak, to ride bikes, to tie our shoelaces, the color of the sky. My father's greatest lesson was that my little body was his plaything and that I had no say over it.

Sexual abuse not only robs us of our basic capacity to feel worthwhile, but it can also leave us open to further violations. Often, when our body has been compromised, our ability to muster the courage to say no to ongoing abuse is weakened or confused. Furthermore, victims may convince themselves that they are deserving of ongoing abuse.

Thinking upon this, I came to the painful realization that I did not have the opportunity to form real sexual boundaries from the start, having been abused at the age of four. The fact was that this first defilement lingered on in my subconscious.

A dirty little script had been planted in my head. It told me that "I am damaged. I am bad, so treat me badly." Like a moth to a flame, I was trapped in my own self-fulfilling prophesy of abuse, eventually morphing into destructive cycles of promiscuity.

It is of little wonder by my late teens, I perceived myself as weak and unable to fend off unwanted sexual attention. It would be untrue to suggest that all my relationships were unhealthy. However, there were clearly situations when I was unable to deal with particular unwanted sexual encounters.

At these times, all I could muster was the ability to build an imaginary force field around my skin, while remaining silent and physically disconnected from my body. All the while, I screamed inside my head, "No! No! No!"

My life had turned into some kind of sordid stage show, and I was always the leading actress with "my men" as a constantly changing cast of actors. Yet whoever was in the support role, the script of abandonment and betrayal remained the same.

There has been too much prejudice and misunderstanding around sexual abuse. I have often heard, even from my friends, "Why did you have sex with him? Why didn't you just say no?" The answer is simple. I froze. I surrendered my body to get it over and done with. I felt powerless, just like I did as a child.

Exercise

Where in your body were you violated sexually? I want you to whisper into these places the word, "No."

Continue to say it softly but firmly over and over: "No, no, no."

Now close your eyes and put your hand on these parts of your body. Fill your thoughts with a deep sense of compassion and understanding for yourself. Let it radiate outward like a bright light touching these parts of your body, one by one. Feel the growing strength within, against those feelings of the past and possibly the future.

Let's do a tap.

Tapping Script 7

KC   Even though my personal boundaries were violated, I love and accept myself. I am still a beautiful person.

KC   Even though I feel stripped, bare, and broken, I will surround my body with a protective light of strength and acceptance.

KC   Even though the boundaries of my [insert abused body part or parts] were violated against my will, I love my body.

EB   My inner child.

SE   So vulnerable.

UE   So broken.

UN   It is safe to let it all go now.

CH   Let go of the tears. Let go of the fear.

CB   I honor and say all the no's that never were expressed.

UA   I honor and say the no's that would have protected you.

TH   I honor and release all the unexpressed no's from my violated body.

EB   No.

SE   No.

UE   I say no.

UN   I shout no!

CH   I freely say no.

CB	I freely shout *no*!
UA	No, no, no.
TH	My little body says *no*!

EB	It is safe to say no to you, [name the person].
SE	It is safe to shout *no* to you, [name the person].
UE	No! No! No!
UN	No! No! No!
CH	No! No! No!
CB	And never again!
UA	*No* to all you people, [name the people].
TH	I am not alone. I am not vulnerable anymore.

[Breathe deeply now and have a sip of water. Say quietly and calmly.]

EB	I am safe.
SE	I can say no as often as I want.
UE	No, no, no …
UN	I can take my time in choosing whom I want to be with.
CH	I have all the power now.
CB	I am in charge of my body.

UA	I am in charge of my emotions.
TH	I am in charge of my sex.
EB	I am in charge of my body's boundaries.
SE	I stand for me now.
UE	Your power is broken.
UN	Soon to be forgotten.
CH	I receive all this healing.
CB	With an open heart.
UA	I will stand strong.
TH	And I will say no!

Place your hand on your heart and repeat three times,

Thank you, body, for receiving this healing.

I know you have endured so much.

Thank you, body, for receiving this healing.

I know you have endured so much.

Thank you, body, for receiving this healing.

I know you have endured so much.

In my early twenties, it became clear to me that my hidden traumas had become a kind of sexual magnet to abusers, who seemed to be able to sniff out my brokenness. Though I provide several examples of the latter half of this chapter, I have given special focus to my relationship with my Reiki therapist, since it best illustrates the physical and psychological impact of my past abuse.

To begin with, this particular situation is unique in that this was with a woman who I held no sexual attraction towards. She had employed me as a receptionist in her clinic but I was also her client. In so many ways, this woman was a lifeline to me who lavished spiritual nourishment upon me, as well as welcomed me into her family and home. I loved and trusted her.

Initially, I considered this a positive mother/daughter relationship, something I had not experienced with my own biological mother. As it turned out, however, she would be just another predator, striking me at my most vulnerable.

In hindsight, it is easy to condemn myself for letting this happen and for not standing up to her. Was I just a fool? Were all her ideas about holistic therapy and healing deceitful and worthless as well? Was I just another victim to a cult of belief, too naïve to unmask the reality of her true intent? The abuse I was suffering not only violated my body but challenged the very premise upon which I had built my own values and beliefs.

When I discovered she was having an affair with a woman outside of her marriage, the penny finally dropped about the true nature of her sexuality, leaving me feeling used and betrayed. It was like a time bomb had been set inside of me and it was only a matter of time before it would go off.

Since the age of four, I have been an asthmatic. It appears to have begun when I started having nightmares after being sexually abused by my cousin. Though my asthma could be attributed to a range of things, my biggest trigger was being emotionally overwhelmed. This resulted in several severe attacks in my childhood requiring significant medical intervention.

Though I did not realize it at the time, my work setting had taken on many of the same characteristics as my home environment when I was twelve years old. Just like my drunken father fondling me on his lap, my trusted therapist was getting me to engage in activities that were clearly a form of sexual misconduct.

She had first approached me sexually during one of our supposed therapy sessions. At the time, I framed her advances and requests to engage with her physically as a gift of intimacy, and I therefore continued to see her under these circumstances. And so, I clung to the notion that this was a more advanced aspect of healing, reserved for her inner sanctum, those that were most "special".

This all led to a kind of "spiritual freeze." I had begun to act in congruence with my own personal demons, whereby I felt less and less in control of my body making the therapist's abuse almost acceptable. It was as if I were keeping a secret from myself, just as my little girl kept secrets from the family, all those years ago.

Reflecting upon it all now, I can see that I had a kind of guru fixation upon this therapist, causing me to place her needs over mine—which as it would turn out, would bring about my own potential demise.

Following on from one of these so-called therapy sessions at work, I began experiencing some level of discomfort with my breathing. Using my asthma pump, I tried to keep my air passages open to continue working. But as the day progressed, I kept pausing between my words while speaking or answering the phone.

At this point, the asthma pump was not having any impact, and I had no idea my oxygen levels were rapidly dropping by the hour. Like the little girl of the past, I was unable to recognize the crisis I was in.

Nonetheless, I continued to do my work duties and, even though I was scared of what was happening to me, I managed to finish my shift and make my way home.

When I finally made it to my apartment front foyer, I looked at the mirror placed on the wall. I was shocked to see a fragile, pale woman looking back at me. My youthful rosy complexion was completely gone. I stood there a full minute thinking, *Wow, I really do look sick.* It suddenly dawned on me that my appearance was similar to when I left my therapy sessions: shocked, slow moving, and crouched over.

I was really struggling to breathe, having only walked up two flights of stairs. Pulling out my keys I struggled to open my door, my hand clearly trembling at this point. The only thought I had was to go to bed, not ring an ambulance or call for any help. I just wanted to go to sleep and make it all go away. When I finally opened the door and entered, something remarkable happened. A distinct, clear voice spoke to me inside my head.

It said, "If you close the door behind you, you will die."

Perhaps it was something genuinely spiritual or just a protective aspect within my mind. Either way, I was no longer overwhelmed by my fear to seek help. This time, I took action to protect myself. Yet in my delirium, I still had not fully comprehended how much danger I was in. Subsequently, I called my sister instead of an ambulance, and she took me directly to the hospital.

Once I was in their care, I finally realized the seriousness of my situation. In fact, the medical staff were quite angry with me having not recognized the symptoms of a serious asthma attack. It was while I was attached to an oxygen machine that I came to the realization that my swollen, inflamed lungs were a symbolic reminder of my own frozen voice, which left me unable to speak out for so long.

It seems incredible now that I had reached such a state of disempowerment, that I had almost died, having considered myself too inconsequential to seek urgent medical attention.

Yet a seed of hope had been planted that day. God, the universe, or perhaps my own desperate inner soul had told me not to close the door. And so, I found a voice where there had not been one before. Though I still continued to struggle with the ravages of my past abuse, the voice I found that day stands by me and for me. For it spoke, and I listened.

I have remained spiritually connected to that voice all my life, despite myself, despite the abuse that had been done to me. For there is one simple message it brings: "I am worth the next breath!"

Exercise

I understand that this is an unknown or unique experience for some, but can you recall an occasion when something deep inside spoke to you—perhaps a time of deep distress or during a near-death experience like mine? If so, consider what was said and why. Perhaps using meditation, ask this voice for ongoing wisdom and guidance.

Here is my example.

To Myself and the Inner Voice,

I am so grateful that you spoke to me. I was feeling very alone and unable to speak up for myself. You spoke up for me, to me. You stopped the door from closing. I am listening to you now with every breath I take. I will continue to remember and honor our connection.

Love, Brigit

Even if you have not had this kind of experience, try to envisage what your inner voice would say to you. How might it warn you or identify your own afflictions in terms of your abuse? Breathe deeply, and pause for a moment.

Now, let's do some tapping about this wonderful gift we have been blessed with—life.

<u>Tapping Script 8</u>

KC   Even though I have been betrayed many times, I trust, love, and accept myself.

KC   Even though there has been times I have been close to giving up on life, I am grateful for every day I have continued to live.

KC   Even though I wondered at times, *Why am I here?* I still love and honor my spirit.

EB   I am safe.

SE   I have a higher purpose.

UE   I will be my higher purpose.

UN   My spirit is kind.

UC   It *is* okay.

CB   I will stay connected.

UA   And choose life above all things.

TH   I celebrate my life now.

EB   I will live with grace and dignity.

SE   I will share my love with others.

UE	As others share their love with me.
UN	I will make myself ready.
CH	Ready to belong.
CB	Because I belong.
AH	Because we belong.
TH	Together.

EB	I choose to be connected to my spirit.
SE	I choose to listen to my intuition.
UE	I choose to speak up.
UN	I choose to protect my body.
UC	I am worth it.
CB	I will keep myself safe now.
UA	I am worth it.
TH	I am worth the call for help.

I would like to tell you, dear reader, that the abuse stopped, that this experience with my therapist leading to a near death would somehow snap me out of further abusive situations arising. But that would be a lie. In my silence, I had become almost complicit in allowing the abuse to gain a foothold in my life.

For me, this had created an ongoing imbalance of power in my most intimate relationships. I found myself choosing to always trust my lovers, believing they would care for me unconditionally, as a friend and perhaps a soul mate.

In truth, I was waiting for a surrogate father who would rescue me from my past childhood suffering and protect me from any future abuse, someone who would care for me as an equal partner.

However, this goal has proven elusive—from being groped by a male work colleague after being followed into the female toilets through to my married boss inviting me on a holiday with him alone. I was continually sexually targeted throughout my adult life. I was even invited by a psychologist who was treating me for post trauma after a serious car accident, to visit his holiday house while his wife and kids were overseas.

And so it went, on and on. Those I trusted and who had economic power over me sought to exploit me in order to fulfil their own sexual gratification. Eventually, I began to gauge my own sense of self-worth in accordance with the value my abusers placed upon me.

I came to accept this as just normal behavior from men, particularly in the workplace. And so, I never considered it as an option to report them for what would now be considered serious acts of sexual misconduct.

It is heartening that there are now greater social awareness and workplace safeguards, protecting us from these kinds of predatory behaviors. Thankfully, the #MeToo movement is giving women, in particular, the moral support to report harassment and sexual assault. However, despite legislative action and growing social awareness, much more work needs to be done.

To truly move forward, we must still overcome the great deceiver, our own inner critic, which undermines and allows us to remain predisposed to such abuses. For it is a hateful, spiteful voice that can often create the notion that we somehow deserved what has happened to us, that what is happening is normal and tolerable, that we were somehow asking for it anyway.

In the end, the truth can become so distorted in our minds that we begin to even doubt our own authentic voice, that which we truly are. So have no illusions. What is asked of you is no easy thing; for some of us, it is even insurmountable. But we must try. We must at least attempt to take back our dignity and personal power. In turn, we must reinforce what is equal, what is just, and what is fair in our lives. Only then can the real healing begin.

<u>Tapping Script 9</u>

KC   Even though it was not safe for me to speak up and tell the truth, I love and forgive myself.

KC   Even though I feared I could lose my job if I spoke up, I love and forgive myself.

KC   Even though I measured my self-worth through the actions of those who sought to exploit me, I love and forgive myself.

EB   I cannot change the past.

SE   I can only change the future.

UE   I forgive myself for past decisions.

UN   I forgive myself completely.

CH   I forgive myself for staying silent.

CB   I forgive myself for never making a stand.

UA   I will no longer be the silent child.

TH   They will no longer have power over me.

EB	I will stand in my own power, for it is strong and it is honest.
SE	I will feel the value of my own power, for it is just, and it is kind.
UE	I know the value of my own voice, for it will only tell the truth now.
UN	I will never be silent again!
CH	I am worth so much more.
CB	I deserve a safe working environment.
UA	I am worth it.
TH	This is basic human dignity, and I deserve it.

EB	I will follow my intuition.
SE	I will listen to my own authentic voice.
UE	I will never settle for less.
UN	That time is over.
CH	That time is gone.
CB	If they cannot hear.
UA	I will make them listen.
TH	I am worthy of much more.

I think, at this point, I need to say there is no such thing as a quick fix to the damage from any form of sexual abuse. Even in my own direct experience, I still struggle to say no to unwanted sexual advances. Perhaps like me, you think, *I should be in control by now! I am an adult, not* a little girl anymore. I have a job. I can run a business. I have raised a family, and so on.

Added to this is a desire to maintain the respect and dignity of a friend or relation who has overstepped the boundaries of acceptable social interaction. This could come in the form of touch, caressing, or kissing that is something more than just friendly.

It is in these muddied circumstances that consent to engage in sexual activity or touching is perhaps misunderstood or confused. Don't be confused. Permission is permission. So often, a look, gesture, or word is somehow interpreted as so much more. But we need not be apologetic if others' needs cannot be met. The consent sought and offered must be given in a mutual and unambivalent manner. In this way, we protect ourselves from feeling upset or violated.

In responding to low-level inappropriate sexual activity, a clear, well-articulated verbal or written message may be enough to alert the enactor that his or her actions are out of line. (I purposely use the word *enactor* to make the discernment that the person's actions may have been deluded rather than abusive.) Obviously, if the behavior is ongoing or your concerns are dismissed, you may need to engage in more strident remedies to address the situation.

My upbringing and my inner critic still whisper to me that maybe I am being too fickle, too precious in how I deal with these issues. I know for a fact that I have been overly cautious or judgmental in how I assessed my expectations of others in the past. Yet I have overcome too much to start second-guessing my actions again and investing trust where it is not deserved or respected. I guess the devil is in the details. Experience and intuition have taught me that seemingly harmless or misconstrued actions can be indicators of a deeper level of misunderstanding or disrespect for sexual boundaries.

In finishing, it has taken a lot of time, effort, and grace to reach this point in my life. It has led me through a maze of confusion, tears, and pain. Yet I have finally arrived at a place of greater wholeness and self-determination. This part of my journey still continues with all its ups and downs. Yet I take comfort in the fact that it is entirely my own, as will be its ultimate destination.

Ritual

> Light a candle to your inner child and say,
>
> Blessed be, little one.
>
> You are worthy of love.
>
> You are safe within my arms.
>
> Now and for always.
>
> Blessed be, little one.
>
> I will protect you now.
>
> And forever.
>
> Blessings on us.
>
> Let's celebrate life.
>
> We are both worthy.

CHAPTER 6
BEYOND THE VICTIM

THIS SHORT CHAPTER explores my own notions of victimhood in relation to my sexual abuse and how it shaped my expectations towards my family and society as a whole. *Victim* is a word that is often bandied about for a range of political and socially motivated purposes. In my case, it is simply one part of my journey from a state of delusion and powerlessness into an authentic sense of self, beyond my abuse.

It would be nice to think that we could all be up front and simply say, "I never asked to be violated, so why should I feel like a victim?"

There is a fine line in establishing a clear path forward to a healthy outcome from the effects of our abuse, and creating a victim mentality that cripples our ability to take responsibility for ourselves.

For me, a victim mentality is one in which an individual's personality traits can manufacture a universal, all-pervading sense of entitlement to justice or compensation. The likely result is that these needs will not be fully met, ending up in an array of negative choices and outcomes throughout our lives. We are then shaped by these circumstances, further justifying that we have been badly done by.

In addition to this, the process of seeking assistance, in itself, can also be very daunting since we are hardly going to shout from the rooftops, "Hey, somebody! I'm a victim over here! Help me! Save me!"

There is more gray than black and white when it comes to the tricky topic of victimhood. In my case, my entire childhood was influenced by an ongoing state of abuse that was systematic and insidiously tolerated by my parents. Of course, this was shaping who I was becoming. There is no question here that I was a victim and blame lay with the adults who should have cared for and protected me. Full stop.

But as an adult, I am now resourced enough to give myself the nourishment and tools to navigate my way back into empowerment. This means moving forward beyond the abuse, beyond being just another victim of life.

Somewhere, at some point, life deals out a series of opportunities or events that challenge the premise for preserving unresolved issues of abuse. For if we do not begin to address our states of perpetual pain and shame, we risk turning into whiners and moaners who blame our abuser, and life generally, for all our woes.

For me, my life choices were beginning to be dictated by my own learned helplessness. It was as if an invisible hand was at play that made all the decisions for me, leaving me open to constant exploitation and abuse. The truth is I was subtly encoded to identify with a victim mentality, so much so that I remained in a kind of hermetically sealed state of post-traumatic stress that could have potentially lingered for a lifetime.

Added to this was an unconscious part of me that yearned for a kind of miraculous reckoning, seeking support as well as compensation for what was done to me.

It took a serious car accident in my twenties and the impact of my physical injuries to finally experience the support that my inner child needed long ago. First at the scene of my accident were the police, which is what the four year old girl had craved for herself all those years earlier. This was followed by the ambulance officers who took me to the hospital, and then the doctors and nurses who washed, fed, and medicated me that simultaneously touched her needs deep within. Finally, my injured body was pinned back together in a six-hour operation, whereupon I would eventually receive a full hip replacement.

Lawyers were principally the source of my retribution. They sought financial compensation on my behalf from the "abuser." And even though the other driver was not a sexual predator, nonetheless, that person had become a kind of scapegoat for all of my miseries, both past and present. In my shock and delirium, I concluded that, at long last, someone was 'gonna' pay!

Though one thing had nothing to do with the other, it is a demonstration of how we can link, and perhaps even attract, events in our life that we can track back to our original abuse. In the end each of our pathways into healing are completely unique.

Exercise

Take some time now. Close your eyes, and imagine this scene playing out. You are in a hospital or a place you associate with healing. Imagine yourself surrounded by fully trained carers who know exactly how to help you heal the pain and suffering of your past abuse. Visualize a blanket being placed around you and your body being washed down.

Feel fluffy white pillows being placed behind your head and the freshly ironed linen warming your body. Next to your bed are beautiful freshly cut flowers given to you by someone who dearly cares about you. Now administer your own self-care by moving through each of the tapping points on your body or using the previous tapping script.

Take note of your breathing, feel it slowly calming you down. Like any victim of a serious injury, realize that you are entitled to be comforted and restored to good health. Your abuse is no exception. Feel the deep, attentive kindness of your carers, knowing you do not need to stay silent and carry the burden of your injuries alone.

It is understandable that we have an ongoing desire for justice, as well as the eventual promise of safety for our body, mind, and spirit. These yearnings can become acute when we have neither a nourishing family environment nor the right therapeutic tools to make positive life choices. Subsequently, we view every circumstance through the lens of our past abuse, long after the situation has changed or is non-existent.

Thus, we remain eternally on guard against any future wrongdoings, each action and word adjudged through this filter. And so, our primitive brain hunts for the next crouching tiger, ready to pounce. The truth is we cannot live a safe, full, and nurturing life maintaining this kind of vigilance.

Another wake-up call of sorts came for me when I was in a therapy session, while I was bemoaning how I was being treated badly by a friend in terms of our comparative financial circumstances.

The therapist, not one to mince her words, basically said that the other person had it a lot worse than I did and that I was playing the victim. This triggered in me a level of sudden self-reflection, as if a mirror had been held up to me, revealing the warts and blemishes of my ill will and self-righteousness.

Upon careful reflection, I came to the conclusion that this was but one more situation, whereby I was viewing supposed violations or wrongdoing through the lens of my past abuse. I realized that I was identifying as a victim under every circumstance, since this is what my abuse had shaped me into, long after its effects had become irrelevant and, in part, nonexistent.

This may be tough to hear if it applies to you too, but if we are to begin to honor our inner child and find a way back to our authentic selves, we must hear it. The angels of self-righteousness that helped us stand up to our abuse can also become our own personal demons of victimhood, if we do not acknowledge their used-by date in our lives.

For many of us, we have an unquenchable need to lock away the perpetrator and throw away the key. However, it is simply not permissible in civilized societies to exact these kinds of punishments. Instead, we again must turn to our professional carers: the police, lawyers, and judges to decide upon a just outcome with impartiality and deference.

Exercise

Write down a list of all the people who have abused you or have caused you harm. Do you need or have you sought retribution or compensation for these abuses? Do you consider them resolved? What other kinds of support have you received? From whom?

The following script seeks to address the desire for the justice and retribution that has perhaps eluded us both in the past and in the present.

Let us begin tapping.

<u>Tapping Script 10</u>

KC   Even though my primitive brain remains on "high alert" for any further threats of abuse, I will begin to open myself to grace and acceptance.

KC   Even though I have spent my life hating my abuser(s), I love and accept who I am.

KC   I am willing to consider I no longer seek an "eye for an eye" for the crimes committed against me.

EB   So much fear for far too long.

SE   So much hate for far too long.

UE   I want to break them! I want to hurt them!

UN   I want them to feel the pain I have felt for a lifetime.

CH   I want to [name any additional punishments you wish to inflict upon them].

CB   It is safe for me to be this angry.

UA   It is time to get this out.

TH   It feels so good to get it out!

EB   Now I must rise.

SE   Now I must be more.

UE   It's time for me to align with love.

UN   Let love grow.

CH   Let it expand to others.

CB   I long to speak from a place of love.

UA   And not my hate.

TH   I can do this.

EB   I choose to imprint my soul with love.

SE   I choose to imprint love upon my inner child.

UE   This hate.

UN   This fear.

CH   It serves no purpose.

CB   I now choose love.

UA   Because I have lived with pain for so long.

TH   I choose to let it all go.

EB   I release myself from fear.

SE   I release myself from the terror.

UE   I release myself into my own protection.

UN   My inner child will be safe.

CH   I know this now.

CB   I choose abundance.

UA   I choose the life I want.

TH   I am safe.

EB   I am safe to do so now.

SE   Let me be free.

UE   From my abuser's words.

UN   From my abuser's body.

CH   My body is mine.

CB   And I am big enough to take it back now.

UA   I trust in grace.

TH   I trust in myself.

For many of us, we remain mentally "frozen out" of the true reality of things and, sadly, our true selves. Sometimes, we are fated to rerun the same victim fight-flight-freeze responses time and time again, so much so that our abnormal becomes our normal.

So, if this sounds like you, *be kind to yourself*. It is a hard path to tread, finding a point of give and take between seeking natural, healthy nourishment and adopting a victim mentality towards life. Also remember, there is much work to be done, and you have only begun.

Exercise

Do you think that your abuse permeates other aspects of your life? Try to name these areas. Write down the thoughts and feelings associated with each of these areas in one column. In another column next to each statement, reframe them in a way that is more positive and objective.

For example, "I hate my boss" becomes "My boss is clearly unhappy. He triggers in me, feelings of anger and abandonment. Much like how [name your abuser] treated me."

Now let's tap again.

Tapping Script 11

KC   Even though I have been violated and abused against my will, I still deeply and completely love and accept myself.

KC   Even though I am a victim of abuse, I still know I'm a good person.

I See You

KC   Even though I am a victim of sexual abuse, I have the right to a happy and healthy life.

EB   I need to heal.

SE   It was not my fault.

UE   Yet I carry the scars.

UN   Yet I carry the memories.

CH   I carry them alone.

CB   They continue to shape my life.

UA   So I will take my life back.

TH   You, [name abuser], have no part in my life anymore.

EB   So I will stand tall.

SE   I will not be your victim.

UE   Not for you or anyone, anymore.

UN   You no longer have power over me.

CH   I will stand tall.

CB   I am in safe hands now.

UE   I will stand tall.

TH   I will create my own safety.

EB	I will live my life well.
SE	I deserve nothing less.
UE	I will seek healing.
UN	This is my right.
CH	You who were once so powerful.
CB	No longer have power over me anymore.
UA	You who have hurt me so badly.
TH	Cannot hurt me anymore!

Well done!

Now take a deep breath. Return to your inner light. Imagine it again filling you up as a cleansing force in your mind, body, and spirit. Feel the pain and trauma subside. Feel it release the old wounds. You are free to let go, and let love in.

Ritual

Light your candle.

Place an offering for your inner child on your altar and say,

You are safe.

Safe to grow happy.

It's time.

Time to grow.

Beyond the wounds.

Beyond the old hate.

That consumed you.

We shall be at peace.

All is safe.

All is sound.

CHAPTER 7
MY BODY, MY LOVE

OUR BODY HAS a language. It speaks to us using pain and other sensations instead of words. In its own way, it maps out our struggles and traumas within our own unique physiology. Like any story, the body naturally seeks a resolution in the form of a healing of both mental and physical ailments.

Scientists have found that physical ailments and injuries can set off a "genomic storm" in our cells that can have a serious effect upon the immune system. A major body trauma, for example, can affect 80 percent of our normal cell functioning. Obviously, this impact can extend beyond the physical to our psychological state of mind.

Louise Hay is a remarkable woman who dedicated many years to helping the sick. This is demonstrated in her book *You Can Heal Your Life*, whereby she establishes a clear link between our thoughts, feelings, and given medical disorders. By consciously looking at what is going on in our bodies, we can create the necessary means to view it in an objective, transparent manner.

In short, every body tells a story of our past pain and suffering.

Ancient tensions and stress built up in the body over time can be unraveled, revealing hidden layers of comprehension and knowledge within ourselves. Essentially, the safer we feel in our skin, the better our chances of warding off or understanding the negative aspects of our life.

When I reflect back upon my own early childhood, I realize just how locked down my little body was. The main way I was physically expressing this was wetting the bed almost every night.

My body was saying, "I'm afraid, and I am not safe," because of the abuse it had incurred. This didn't change until my young teenage mind provided the means to cast off these behaviors, as the social pressures of my adolescent years closed in on me.

The question I ask myself now is "Did my terror and shame associated with my abuse simply disappear, or did it manifest itself in another condition or illness somewhere else in my body?" My answer to this is an emphatic "yes" to the latter.

In truth, all I succeeded in doing was suppressing my natural responses to trauma, which were triggered in the form of eyelash pulling, bedwetting, and asthma attacks. Though I have never fully recalled the events of my abuse as a four year old, I know, deep in my core, that they are linked with each of these physical reactions. The fact of the matter is repressed memories are a recognized medical condition, often compared to dissociative amnesia.

For some of us, we may spend a lifetime masking the root mental causes of our sickness through remedies and medications. But there is a substantial body of medical evidence indicating that there are identifiable symptoms of trauma in given parts of the body that go beyond any normal, understandable explanation.

In my case, the phrase, "to feel it in your bones" seems quite apt, since I believe the body does not erase the evidence of unprocessed abuse and trauma. Instead, an imprint is left in the unconscious memory. Somehow, a healthy process must be established whereby a meeting of mind and body can be fully understood and the pain released permanently.

By tapping into the body's latent abilities to heal itself, we are not entirely reliant upon extrinsically administered medical remedies and cures. In this way, therapeutic techniques like EFT have the potential to unlock these sources of data, opening up our body's meridians much like a valve on a tap.

Exercise

Write down those physical ailments that you suspect are linked to your suppressed unconscious memory.

Where are they in your body? Why do you think they are there? What events do you believe they are linked to? What events or actions continue to trigger these physical responses?

Sometimes, a mild illness or ailment may force us to rest or reconsider our priorities in life. This may prompt an internal dialogue in terms of how our state of mind is impacting upon our bodies. Other times, significant traumas may crack open that which has remained dormant in our subconscious.

As discussed in the previous chapter, this occurred for me after my car accident. My instant reaction was that I was left vulnerable and frightened, feeling like a helpless newborn babe. Throughout the accident, my fight-flight response induced a heightened sense of consciousness, causing me to retain every aspect of my ordeal in incredible detail.

I remember the other car not giving way to me in an intersection. It felt like minutes as I watched it plough into my car, causing it to spin like a top. In that moment, I was acutely aware of the lack of control I had, a sensation that was strangely familiar, as if I had been in this place before.

Yet again, my mind was frozen and my body broken. The accident was significant; the medical attention was immense. Even though I was blameless, I could feel the old patterns related to my previous abuse arising in me again.

Exercise

Perhaps you may have encountered a similar kind of situation or a minor trauma. Think upon this, and write down those associated events in relation to past abuse and abandonment issues.

Try the following tapping script to release some of the trauma that may still be locked in your body.

Tapping Script 12

KC   Even though my body has borne the brunt of my abuse, I love and accept who I am.

KC   Even though I haven't felt safe and connected with my body, I profoundly love and accept myself.

KC   Even though my body has tried to "speak" to me with its fear, its shame, I will now listen to it with an open heart.

EB   My story.

SE   I still feel the pain of my story in my [identify body part].

UE   My words.

UN   I still feel the pain of the words in my [identify body part].

CH   My fear.

CB   I still feel the fear trapped in my [identify body part].

UA   My shame

TH   I still feel the shame trapped in my [identify body part].

EB   It is frozen there.

SE   In these places.

UE	My body has paid the price.
UN	It's time to take it back.
CH	Into new healing.
CB	Into new growth.
UA	Into every cell.
TH	My body deserves to be whole again.

EB	It has been too long, my body.
SE	Too much fear.
UE	Too much shame.
UN	It is time for you to speak.
CH	You have been silent for far too long.
CB	You will be safe again.
UA	It is time to be safe.
TH	You have always deserved more.

EB	I am taking you home.
SE	I am taking you into my care.
UE	I will caress your skin.
UN	I will bathe your wounds.

CH   You are with me now, my body.

CB   In me.

UA   About me.

TH   My body, my love.

Other echoes of abuse resonated through my body as I began to intuit tangible links between the accident and my repressed memories about my cousin's abuse. In trying to recall what he did to me, I was aghast to find that it was sweet memories that first flooded into my mind.

I remember loving my eighteen-year-old cousin very much. A clear example of this is the special feelings of the honor and privilege I felt being taken for a drive with him in his new sports car, something he did not do with any of my siblings.

However, I do not remember the drive itself, which is strange, considering how vividly I recall the green color of his car and the distinct smell of the leather seats. It is as if this part of the movie tape had simply been cut from my mind's eye. What did transpire immediately after this event were reoccurring childhood nightmares of being pursued by a man in my cousin's home.

I saw a man with a bow and arrow hunting me down in order to kill me. Notably, the bow and arrow had the ability to find me no matter what twists or turns I made in order to avoid it. Inevitably, I would awake in a terrified state, sitting in a pool of my own urine.

Over time, I came to understand the arrow represented the piercing, violent nature of my cousin's sexual penetration. While I had blotted out the actual events, my unconscious mind took me to the scene of the crime over and over again, trying to somehow reconcile this violation.

For so long, this hidden abuse was locked away in a kind of tomb of silence, left to fester and finally manifest in my physical and psychological states. Yet no noise, no scream would ever emanate from my lips during the nightmares I had, as if the secret was trapped within me, like a hostage. Somehow, I had become responsible for my own misery, or perhaps I had been threatened into silence.

In my late twenties, I remember experiencing a severe tightness in my throat while broaching the subject of my cousin in a therapy session. My therapist directed me to release the silence surrounding this event through a primal scream. What emanated from my mouth was a shrill, unearthly noise that I associated more with a hysterical child than a full-grown adult woman.

The shocking conclusion was that this tightness, along with other associated asthma symptoms, might be linked to gagging on my cousin's penis while he was forcing fellatio upon me.

Other questions emerged. How did I come to love him in a way that can only be described as romantic at the age of four? What does that even mean? The only logical conclusion was that these feelings were encouraged, procured in my young, impressionable mind.

He gave me compliments that I had never heard before in my life. He told me I was pretty, sweet, a kind girl, and so on. This fed the hunger, the starving heart that yearned for these words to come from anybody, especially my parents.

What I had now come to understand is that I had been groomed by my cousin. He was the adult, I was not. He knew what he was doing.

Upon arriving at this conclusion, I also realized why the accident had been so traumatically familiar to me: my cousin had abused me in his car.

The next time I recall being in his company was when I was eight years old and I remember feeling ugly, ashamed and fearful. I can now make the association that the eyelash pulling was my little girls attempt to try to relieve some of the symptoms of fear and the bed wetting was an unconscious attempt to tell those around me that I had been a victim of sexual abuse.

I stood in my aunties loungeroom feeling that it was my fault I was no longer the pretty girl for him. I thought I had failed him.

My suffering was further intensified by my mother's frustration, which focused upon my trichotillomania and bedwetting. This resulted in direct or indirect shaming. I remember that I had to wear buttoned up gloves to bed so that my small fingers couldn't pull at what was left of my tiny eyelashes. I felt different to the rest of my family, an alienation that validated my preexisting conditions. It's just so sad.

The unremitting pressure of dealing with my shame forced my personal value to splinter off from me. My value then became a dislocated entity, and I was a gypsy in my own body, and in my own mind.

Such was the intensity of re-establishing a healthy sense of identity and well-being. It was at this time I came to acknowledge that my mother was too emotionally ill-equipped to deal with what was happening to me, even though I was only four years old. I was hoping for the soft call of "Mother" to guide me out of the dark forest and protect me from my abuser. But, of course, none of this happened. It all felt predestined, as if it was something I had to endure, part and parcel of my own unique circumstances. Perhaps I even deserved it?

But this would not be my lot in life. I would not let myself be trapped in this learned helplessness. The old narrative that the abuse was my fault had held sway over my life for far too long. The truth as I had come to understand it was that *I was groomed, and none of this was my fault.*

Time to throw this story out! Let's tap.

Tapping Script 13

KC   Even though I carry in my body and mind the belief that the abuse was my fault, I still love and accept who I am.

KC   Even though I blamed and labeled myself as weak, I love and accept who I am.

KC   As an adult, I now know the truth.

EB   It was not my fault.

SE   I was groomed.

UE   It was not my fault.

UN   I was set up.

CH   It was not my fault.

CB   I was used.

UA   It was not my fault.

TH   I was just an innocent child.

EB   The abuse is not my fault.

SE   It was never my fault.

UE   I should have never been violated.

UN   I should have been protected.

CH   All the shame and blame I carried.

CB   I let it all go.

UA   The perceived weakness in my heart.

TH   I let it all go.

EB   All this judgment.

SE   All this pain.

UE   All this grief.

UN   I need a pathway back.

CH   Back to kindness.

CB   Back to truth.

UA   Back to love.

TH   Back to myself.

EB   I see the truth now.

SE   I am loved.

UE   I am lovable.

UN   I am open to receiving more love.

CH   I am not alone anymore.

CB   I am home, home in my body.

UA   I am valuable.

TH   My value has returned home to me.

EB   My inner child is loved.

SE   I see you.

UE   I see you now.

UN   You are safe with me.

CH   You are safe now.

CB   I am free to love myself.

UA   You are free to love.

TH   Let us love together.

EB   Free from blame.

SE   Free from shame.

UE   We are free now.

UN   I choose to be released from this responsibility.

CH   Because the responsibility was never mine.

CB   That time is over.

UA   I will live my life on my own terms.

TH   I am finally safe to be seen.

Well done!

Really spend some time with yourself releasing any residual grief and pain. Tap as many times as you need to fully reclaim the truth that you did not invite the violation.

In reality, our bodies cannot lie. Like a good friend, it will keep the awful truth from us as long as it can, depositing the pain in different parts of itself. But eventually it will find the right opportunity to speak, even if we are still in denial.

And so I say to you, my body, I am so sorry. I will now honor you. You have stood by me, a silent witness to my pain. It is time for me to stand, to take control, as it cannot come from any other place.

Exercise

Write a letter to your body, as if you were expressing thanks to a friend.

Here's my example:

My Dear Body, My Love,

How do I begin to give thanks to you for carrying me all my life? We have shared so many bumps on the road, yet you have endured so much with me.

My body, my love, you have suffered pain, infections, and illness, a myriad of physical and emotional conditions. Thank you.

My body, my love, you have held shock and trauma in the muscles, bones, joints, sinew, lungs, and organs. You have been waiting patiently for me to express the stories that needed to be shared. Your aches, your pains were always working with me and not against me as I have often thought.

My body, my love, you are on my side. We share a connection that is to be revered and celebrated. We are in a sacred union.

My body, my love, I will not abandon you again. Whenever you send me a sensation of pain, I will sit and hear what you are trying to share with me.

My body, my love, I will commit more to you, more often. You are the temple that houses my soul. You deserve the spiritual worship of tapping and meditation, as well as good, nutritional practices.

My body, my love, you are beautiful exactly as you are, here, in this moment. Thank you for all the pleasure and adventures we have shared together.

My body, my love. May we live a long, healthy, and happy life together.

Love Brigit x

Eventually, it would take many years of expert therapeutic care and resourcing to extract the heavy burden of my abuse. Ultimately, I gave the four-year-old all the compassion, forgiveness, and understanding she so desperately needed.

Tapping Script 14

Tap upon the karate chop (KC) point and say over and over again,

I have come home to my body.

I have come home to my love.

My body, my love,

I have come home to you, my dear.

I am home.

Breathe and feel yourself come into your body, as an equal, as a partner in your life. It is time for you to love your body as it speaks to you. Listen, love, and help your body, as it has been at the front line for too long, doing all the heavy lifting. For many of us, our bodies have endured the harshest judgments, brutal shame, and all manner of defiling acts. It is on us now to take control and care for our beautiful, loyal friend.

When you can, give it a rest from the toxic feelings and thoughts that rob it of its strength and promise. Remember your body is a gift, no matter what anyone has to say about it. Whatever the size, condition, shape, or color, your body is a beautiful, unique creation, and it is perfect for you.

Ritual

Light the candle for your inner child.

Look at your body.

See the child within it.

Caress it.

Feel its warm breath in your nostrils.

Feel its precious heart in your chest.

Feeling the stories within.

Tell your body.

> I love you.

> I feel you.

> I see you.

Chapter 8
Toxic Loyalty

WHEN I WAS around twelve years old, visitors would come to our home for lunch on Sunday, whereupon my father would drink a lot and all day. After all the guests had left, Mum would sit my father up and fill him with cups of tea, trying her best to sober him up.

Dad was another person when he was drunk. While in this state, he would specifically seek me out, his daughter, Brigit. As a young girl, I did not have the power to resist his demands and would sit politely on his lap. Dad would always stink of beer while holding his face close to my mine. As a result, I still cannot tolerate the smell of it to this day.

He would then ask me to tell him how much I loved him, and I would oblige him, though I felt no genuine feeling for him at these times. He would kiss my tightly shut lips far too many times for what was appropriate for a daughter. He would then place his hands down my top, touching my budding young breasts, and sing, "Booby booby doo," over and over again.

I would freeze each time it happened, though I would never complain or call out to my mother, who was always sitting next to us on the couch as it occurred.

This is my secret shame, which I kept to myself for years.

To remain loyal, I reframed the abuse in my mind with such thoughts as, *Dad was just being affectionate, Dad was drunk so it was not his fault*, or *Dad must see me as someone special*. The truth is my own father was a sexual predator, and my mother was his unwitting accomplice.

In my late forties, I knew it was time to act and confront my father about his abuses. It took all my courage and strength to do this, knowing there was a possibility of never being welcomed back into my family home.

Initially, things went well. Upon hearing my concerns, he was immediately remorseful, telling me to, "Let it go." We then hugged, and I felt I had been sincerely met in that moment, grateful that he had finally taken some personal responsibility for his actions.

I left the house that night, feeling lighter and incredibly proud of myself having faced down these demons. However, as time passed, I came to understand that there was an unfulfilled part of me that needed my family to somehow embrace the truth, to understand how much the abuse had shaped my relationship with them and myself.

I then had a disturbing dream about my father. We were both our current ages, and I was sitting on his lap again on a Ferris wheel. He was molesting me again while he sang his dirty little ditty. However, this time, I kept asserting myself over and over, "I am your daughter! I am your daughter! I am your daughter!"

But even then, he would not stop. I realized that he was still the same father of my childhood, now openly ignoring my objections. Even in his eighties, I realized his sickness had not gone. Eventually, I freed myself from him and ran to where the rest of my family were gathered.

"It is happening again!" I declared. "You must stop this!" But none of them responded. None of them even seemed to care. It was as if I weren't there. My father appeared, and I told him that I would kill him if he did not tell the rest of the family the truth.

But he just stared blankly through his drunken eyes and slurred, "You go ahead."

I then realized he would prefer death to my family finding out the truth.

This dream was a reawakening, a means of seeking true resolution from the broken trust and unsaid words of my father. In his sickness, he had imprinted a dysfunctional narrative about the masculine upon my young, impressionable mind, a story of men whereby it was okay for a daughter to be used for sexual gratification. It was a pleasure I must provide to him, giving my father what he wanted, whenever he wanted it. Subsequently, I had passively suffered through this ritualistic abuse, incurring bouts of self-loathing and disassociation, ultimately considering myself too worthless to protect.

As in my dream, I needed my immediate family to know what I had gone through and kept hidden away, all of these years, to remove, once and for all, the stigma of my psychological deficits and other antisocial traits alienating me from my family. Moreover, I needed him to confess to my family so that he would now take on the shame in my heart and place it in his.

However, none of this happened.

Instead, five years after this conversation with my father, he has not mentioned it again, with no inquiry as to how I was now coping, nothing. In fact, what I now believe he meant by, "Let it go" was to forget it ever happened.

But the story has not ended, could not end, here for me. I had resolved to believe I had done all I could to help him reconcile all his poor choices, all his wrongdoings. I now take back control of my own story.

Exercise

Part of the process to reconcile my father's abuse was to write an imaginary letter expressing his contrition for what he had done to me.

Here it is.

> *To dear Brigit, my wife, my daughters, and my sons,*
>
> *I write this letter as evidence that I have wronged my daughter, our beloved Brigit. I have broken my commitment to her, as her father and as a man. I have failed to protect her from the sexual predator within. I have made terrible choices in my drunken state and have betrayed Brigit and this entire family.*
>
> *I have been stupid, selfish, and emotionally weak in failing to stay sober for all of you. My intoxicated state created cracks in my self-control whereby I allowed myself to violate Brigit and deeply impact her ability to trust men.*
>
> *I stand before you pledging to take full responsibility for my actions and will seek the professional help I need so I can earn Brigit's trust and forgiveness.*
>
> *I touched you, Brigit, in a way a father never should. You were not meant to carry the burden of my sexual illness. It was always mine to bear. It is time we, as a family, fully support and nourish you in all the ways you need.*
>
> *Brigit, you are a beautiful woman who deserves a man who will protect and respect you and keep you safe. I have fallen short of this sacred duty. But I vow to honor you now, till the end of my days.*
>
> *Love Dad*

Is it possible for you to ask for such a letter, a letter that expresses forgiveness and regret—not only from the perpetrator but also from those who should have, could have, stopped the abuse.

Perhaps, like me, your only option is to create a letter that seeks to begin your own self-healing.

After writing your letter, you may choose to discuss it with someone who can use it as a means to identify how you can develop strategies to heal from this abuse. You may want to keep it in a private, sacred place. In my case, I keep my letter in a little silk bag on my altar, so the apology is close to my inner child.

Okay, let's do some tapping.

Tapping Script 15

KC	Even though I never received any remorse from [name abuser], I love and accept myself.
KC	Even though [name abuser] will never take responsibility for his or her actions, I love and accept who I am.
KC	Even though I crave an apology from [name abuser], I recognize the suffering it is creating.
EB	I crave an apology so much.
SE	I want so much for the pain to end.
UE	I want [name abuser] to look me in the eyes and say sorry.
UN	I am so angry with [name abuser]!
CH	He or she has the responsibility
CB	To say sorry, just once.
UA	That's all I'm asking for.
TH	Then I can begin to heal.

EB   In my mind.

SE   In my body.

UE   In my spirit.

UN   I have committed myself to this quest.

CH   Whether or not I receive an apology.

CB   It no longer matters.

UA   Because nothing will stop me now.

TH   *I* will choose to heal.

EB   Because *I am* deserving of more.

SE   Though I will never get back what I am owed.

UE   I will go on with my life.

UN   Enough of the loneliness.

CH   Enough of the brokenness.

CB   Enough of the apology.

UA   That will not come.

TH   In this, you have failed me.

EB   In this, you have failed yourself, [name abuser].

SE   It is all on you now and nothing on me.

UE	With or without you.
UN	I have begun.
CH	With or without you.
CB	I will grow strong.
UA	Where I will rise.
TH	You will turn to dust.

EB	Blessings on my mind now.
SE	Because it speaks the truth.
UE	Blessings on my body now.
UN	Because it feels the pain.
CH	Blessings on my soul now.
CB	It above all things.
UA	Deserves a new beginning.
TH	So much wasted time.

EB	So many lost opportunities.
SE	You who have taken so much.
UE	And given so little back.
UE	Let the waters part.

CH   Let me walk free from you now.

CB   You who have defined me by your abuse.

UA   Have no place with me anymore.

TH   No more, no more, no more.

In respect to my cousin, there is little left of the young man I loved once so deeply. When we meet at family functions, there is just an awkwardness whenever we say hello. But we both know we share a hidden history, one that keeps us locked together in shame and in suffering.

So it is I who am left to ponder, *How could I have ever harbored such feelings of loyalty to him and to my father? To let myself become so broken by my silence?* The answer is relatively simple. My young, loving heart had become overladen by a toxic loyalty, born out of a fear of the masculine, the fear of men.

Unfortunately, it has come at a high price. To keep loyal and protect these men, I turned the blame inward, making it all my fault, my sin. Sadly, my experience as a therapist has shown me that this kind of reaction is commonplace among the clients I work with.

Perhaps like me, your younger self only kept the abuse secret as a means of holding on to what love was left in the household. In my case, this person was my own father.

To be so overwhelmed that you cannot speak up, not even to your own mother in fear of her retribution, her abandonment—maybe this sounds all too familiar, something you know well in yourself or have encountered with others?

What a terrible trap for a child!

By not protecting me from his sexual depravities, my father unknowingly wounded my understanding of the masculine. So it is no coincidence that I married a man like my father, with an alcoholic addiction.

My next love after my marriage ended was with a man who asked for an open relationship after two years together, to which I said no. The missing ingredient of unconditional loyalty from the men I have loved remains an open wound, replaying itself over and over again.

It is time to put aside blind faith and obedience. It is time to give loyalty to the one who is owed it the most, she who has endured so much: myself, my inner child. Only then can the real story of restoration begin.

Even as I write these words, I feel an anxiety rising up in my body. It comes in the form of an old loyalty to my family and my origins. It is so powerful I feel it will overcome my adult reasoning. Yet this must all end here and now. I know I am digging down deep here, dear reader, down into buried memories, the old bloodstained earth.

Let's do some tapping.

Tapping Script 16

KC   Even though I am scared to put myself first, I love and accept who I am.

KC   Even though it is foreign for me to put myself first, to speak up without fear of punishment, I love and accept myself.

KC   Even though I have struggled to tell the truth, I love and accept myself and my inner child.

EB	It is safe for me to tell the truth.
SE	It is time for others to hear it.
UE	I must protect myself now.
UN	Blessed be the child who has survived.
UC	I am the child who has survived.
CB	So many of us have our own wounded story.
UA	Let us no longer remain silent.
TH	We owe a debt of loyalty to no one.

EB	It is my inner child that now deserves my loyalty.
SE	It is my inner child that now deserves respect.
UE	Only compassion and love will live here now.
UN	There is no room for anything else.
UC	No one will stop me.
CB	My own grace will be my guiding force.
UA	This is my time of truth now.
TH	I am safe to speak it.

(Repeat the following portion of the script three times.)

EB	It is safe to break the silence.
SE	It is safe to speak the words.
UE	To feel the anger.
UN	To feel the sadness.
UC	To finally, finally, *finally* speak up!
CB	So let me throw away the lock.
UA	And the key.
TH	It is time to begin.

Exercise

Describe in your own words your own life achievements, big and small, beyond that of the abused child of the past. For me, it has been being a loving daughter, a caring mother, a writer, a celebrant, a great omelet maker, a groovy dancer, a successful therapist, and a kind partner (well, sometimes).

Find these things in your own life. Think upon how each of these seemingly ordinary achievements have enriched the tapestry of what is your own unique human existence. Ask yourself, why am I less deserving to be loved and valued? Why have my words or the words of others kept me small for all this time? Why should I live behind a wall of shame and sadness?

Now honor this thought at the altar of your inner child. Remember to say, "I see you." And remind her or him, they are not forgotten. Light a candle at your altar and consider how you will free your inner child from the corrosive effects of this old critical thinking.

Repeat this ritual and process daily, and see where it takes you in your thinking and your general outlook on life.

Some abusers are eventually held accountable. Whether through the legal system or a life haunted by their crimes, a true reckoning can occur. However, whatever the fate of your abuser, the fact of the matter is *you* must choose to heal; *you* must choose to move on.

This can be perceived by some as a weakness or perhaps letting your abuser off the hook. But it is a means of drawing a line under what has been lost and a real demonstration to yourself and others that you are no longer prepared to give them any more. The power that once held sway over you, you have taken back. Subsequently, the effects of your abuse can be gently and methodically dismantled and diffused all together. [We will explore this topic in greater depth in the last chapter].

I say this in the context of working with clients who have never emerged from their pain despite their abusers having passed away or never having taken back responsibility for what they did. It is in our power to recover even without their acknowledgment of their abuse or their remorse.

Please note, I have tried to tread carefully with my own insights and words of advice given in this chapter. I know, from firsthand experience with my clients, the levels of brutality and violation many of you have suffered far exceeds my own personal experiences of abuse. But know I stand by you, because *we must stand together.* So seek out the wisdom and support you need to do this work. And always remember, you are not alone.

Ritual

Light your candle to your inner child.

Honor yourself.

Honor your childhood.

Tell your inner child that he or she has your loyalty.

Tell your inner child that the silent years are over.

Tell them that the past is the past.

And the future is ours.

Love and blessings to you dear child.

CHAPTER 9
THE MOTHER WHO WON'T STAND

AS I SIT here writing this chapter, I have the great fortune to look out at a beautiful mountain, reminding me of the archetypes associated with "the Great Mother," the mother whose clear peak can be seen high above the dark, circling clouds. She stands out like a beacon watching over me, calling me home, the mother who stands tall against the driving winds and rains, soaking up their ferocity so that her lush and abundant fertility can be expressed in the springtide.

Sadly, none of this actually relates to my real mother.

I remember as a young girl placing my head in her lap, hoping she would stroke my hair and forge some kind of intimate connection with me, but it simply didn't happen.

Even her smell came across as harsh and acrid as she constantly reeked of bleach. In this way, she served our family well by creating a clean and hygienic space to live in. Yet I could not but yearn for something beyond this, something nourishing and beautiful that would align us in the feminine and in love. Perhaps it was to do with her own difficult upbringing or modest educational background, but the fact was she just didn't know how to stand by me, especially against the abuse.

My mother did not drink alcohol, yet she was with a man who abandoned himself to it. Maybe this was simply her modus operandi, her lot in life. Looking at old childhood photos of my mother sitting next to my father, I can almost see the impending sense of betrayal and sadness etched into her eyes.

Yet despite what she must have felt, what she must have known, she sat silent as he ran his fingers over me. Trapped like captured prey, I was left in the hands of a molester. And so it was a double horror that unfolded for me, one of torment and confusion toward my father and another of abandonment by my mother. Hence, the words in my young mind were not *Why is he doing this to me?* but *Why isn't she stopping him?*

It is my experience as a therapist that it is not uncommon for the other parent to be nearby as a violation of his or her own child is taking place. Often the reasons given are that the other parent remains unaware or, somehow, not tuned in to what is happening even though he or she may have been literally in the same space.

Sometimes, the other parent becomes paralyzed by fear or denial, as a result of his or her own past history of abuse. Moreover, threats by their spouse to withdraw financial, physical, and emotional security could also be a motivating factor.

It's worth noting that the night I went home to confront my father, I was inadvertently also confronting my mother. This was confirmed when, after receiving my father's apology, I turned to mother and asked her directly, "Did you know Dad was doing this?"

She answered in a high, shrill voice, "No, of course not!"

Even in this moment, I thought she might at least give me a hug, however misguided she thought I had been. But instead the familiar wall of denial and fear was thrown up against me. The child was once again pushed aside, back to somewhere forgotten, away from mother's safe little world.

As with my father, she too never mentioned my conversation again in my company. Like some cold case that the police are simply unwilling to open up, no inquiries or plans to support me were put into place. The sad truth is I didn't believe her, since she was sitting only inches from him during the abuse. As a child, I could see the resentment and tension in her face, for she knew his patterns just as I had come to know them. Yet I was still thrown to the wolves.

Exercise

Do you have a story like this one, of the one who did not stand by you during your abuse? Was it your mother? Was it your father? A sibling? A coach? A teacher? A best friend? Someone you trusted and who was meant to keep you safe but didn't?

What is your relationship with that person now? Has it continued despite the abuse? Could you speak or write a letter to him or her? What would you say?

Tapping Script 17

Okay, let's tap for your inner child and for a little bit of peace.

KC Even though [name the bystander] stayed silent when I needed him or her most, I love and accept who I am.

KC Even though [name the bystander] didn't protect me, I can keep myself safe now.

KC Even though I was abandoned to the abuser, I love and accept myself.

EB This rage.

SE This abandonment.

UE This deep, deep sense of pain.

UN I have felt it for years.

CH	It is safe to name it.
CB	It is safe for me to express it!
UA	[Name the bystander] failed me!
TH	[Name the bystander] didn't stand up for me.
EB	[Name the bystander] could have stopped it!
SE	His or her silence became my silence.
UE	His or her shame became my shame.
UN	Against myself.
CH	Against others.
CB	But now I choose to let it go.
UA	I deserve to be free from my silence.
TH	I deserve to be free from his or her silence.
EB	I can speak up now without fear.
SE	And I can stand for myself and others.
UE	This shall never happen again.
UN	To me or to anyone.
CH	Not on my watch.
CB	All children deserve to be safe.

UA	Safe from all abuse.
TH	All children deserve to be protected.

EB	I now protect the child within.
SE	I will be safe.
UE	He or she will be safe.
UN	Out of harm's way.
UC	They who should have stood up for me.
CB	Are no longer needed.
UA	Let them be silent.
TH	But my silence is over.

Take some time to tap over the preceding script as many times as you need. See yourself taking control and protecting your inner child with each tap, with each statement.

My psyche gifted me with an amazing dream the night before I wrote this chapter. All I had was the title, but the dream gave me the overall flavor of what I would write about.

I am with a group of men, and they are friendly. I feel comfortable. I am not in a relationship, so I feel excited by the romantic possibilities while in their company. As our time comes to a close, one of the men hands me his business card with an address of a café for us to meet for lunch. There is a spontaneous connection to this man, and I come to believe that he could potentially become a long-term soul mate.

When the day arrives to meet him, I eagerly set about getting ready. I check my hair and choose a flattering dress. I also apply my lipstick several times, feeling a genuine sense of nervousness and anticipation.

On the way, I become unsure of where to go, yet I manage to finally move in the right direction. As I am approaching the café, I look down at my feet, and I am stunned to see that I am not wearing shoes. My shock then turns to horror, as I discover that they are not my feet at all but are, in fact, my mother's! I awoke with a start from this dream instantly understanding its meaning: when I meet men, I do so not from my own standpoint (standing on my own two feet), but from that of my mother's standpoint (standing in her feet).

In that moment, a terrible realization took hold of me. Not only had my mother knowingly allowed me to be used and abused by my father, but a neurological pathway had been created in my brain, whereby this extended to all men who sought an intimate relationship with me.

Here I was in my dream, walking toward my potential new lover, mired down in the brokenness and sorrow of my mother's past abandonment. The stains of my abuse, which started on the family couch, had left me vulnerable to further abuse each time I sought an intimate relationship with a man. And so the family disease, the malaise of abuse, had been passed on.

I am still trying to stand on my own two feet now and not my mother's. It is no easy thing to overcome, since those moments on the couch have seeped into my identity, into my very sense of being. It is often said that every one of us needs to stand on our own two feet in life. But we need to first ask ourselves exactly whose feet we are really standing in. Thus, we must come to the very hard task of questioning the very basis upon which we have formulated our beliefs and values.

Exercise

Close your eyes and try to envisage the place, people, and circumstances leading to an abusive event in your past. Put yourself there, as you were, as they were. Think about the people or person who could have stood up to your abuser(s). Feel the thoughts and feelings emerge in your mind and body.

Now get a piece of paper. Using your nondominant hand, write down anything you can think of, in simple, direct, childlike words. It doesn't matter if your ideas are irrational or naïve. Simply jot down whatever comes into your mind about how you were not protected, acknowledged, or supported by them.

Here is my own example for you to consider:

Why isn't my mom standing up for me?

Mom, I'm scared!

Help me, Mommy!

But my mom does not move.

My mom does not speak.

My mommy is not here for me.

Why doesn't she say something?

Why doesn't she slap his face?

She must be hearing his song.

She must know where his hand is going.

She must see his hand on my chest.

She mustn't be able to see him.

She mustn't be able to see me.

My mother does not see me,

but she is looking right at me.

I see it in her eyes!

I see it in her face!

My mom must love my dad more

Because she lets him do this to me.

I cannot stop him.

He is unstoppable.

Maybe all men are unstoppable?

Maybe I can't say no to any man?

Is this right, Mother?

Is this how I should feel?

My mother does not stand by me.

No one stands for me.

She is the mother,

But she is silent.

She must be teaching me to be silent.

I cannot say no to my father

Because he is my father.

I am alone.

So,

I will be numb.

I will be used.

I will mean nothing.

I am …

nothing.

My mother, consciously or unconsciously, allowed me to take on my father like some macabre chore, as if servicing his abuse was part of my household duties. Perhaps she was also acting out of self-preservation, trying to save herself from his predatory nature. It is difficult to know. The only thing I truly understand is that I was left to deal with the full brunt of his sexual cravings.

Needless to say, neither of my parents had the knowhow or moral fortitude to deal with the growing emotional toll it was taking on me as a child. So it just went on, week after week, year after year.

Eventually, this unresolved cycle of abuse spilled over into my marriage, whereby my responsibilities toward my alcoholic, sexually abusive father were replaced by my responsibilities to an alcoholic, emotionally abusive husband.

During the years of my marriage, this sense of duty to men was coupled with a deep anticipatory anxiety whereby I was consistently left wondering, *Is he going to get drunk today? Will he be verbally abusive today?*

Eventually, my sense of responsibility to my husband has carried over into caring for my children, as he was largely unfit to be around them. Now in my mind's eye, it is my ex-husband who sits on the family couch, saying and doing nothing, leaving me to take on all of the financial and emotional responsibility of raising our three boys.

I now know as I continue this quest, this writing, that I will finally peel back the layers of my life, unencumbered by the weight of my parents' negligence and unmet responsibilities. So that one day, the twelve-year-old will be free, no longer a victim, no longer a surrogate wife, no longer a sacrificial lamb.

She will be just as she should be with all the same headaches and everyday responsibilities as everyone else in life. This may not be the most inspiring way to the end this chapter, but it is enough, being normal is enough.

Ritual

Light your candle for your inner child.

It is time to walk on your own two feet.

Tell your inner child.

You will be her mother, you will be his father.

I See You

You are walking with them now.

And for always.

Blessed be.

Blessed be.

Blessed be.

CHAPTER 10
ADDICTION

Part 1: Mother's Milk

It perhaps comes as no surprise that many of us who have been subjected to abuse turn to addictive substances to avoid or quell deep-seated trauma despite its damaging effects upon our health.

Notably, our consumer society has honed in on what we want, or more aptly, what we think we want, including our soft and hard addictions. It is timely then, to begin stripping back what is motivating all these unbridled desires and compulsions, by asking the question, "Why am I so unhappy that I need to yield to these addictions?"

Maybe we should begin to consider what makes us happy and when it first emerged in us in its purest form. I believe our first significant sense of happiness starts with the initial bonds of love we form with our mother.

Our mother, is generally our first human port of call as we transition into this life. All of us, mother and child alike, should feel permitted to seek a close, sustainable bond from this connection, the first of our relationships.

To genuinely be seen, heard, and held at birth is to be loved by the very thing that gave us life, within and beyond the womb. What was once the same as us now holds us, as if we are being embraced by the universe itself. In these first few precious moments, it feels as though no force in existence can break this binding relationship.

Our mother is also our introduction to sensual pleasure, our first spiritual bliss. This can be in the way we feel her breath upon our face, hear her calming voice when we cry, or taste her warm, nourishing milk upon our lips. It is of little wonder that if this intimate bond is broken, we can end up yearning for it for the rest of our lives.

This situation can be further complicated if the mother herself is struggling to emotionally attach to the child. Research tells us that for these women, responding empathetically to their newborn can be fraught with difficulties. Subsequently, the child is at risk of being more vulnerable to a variety of mental health issues, including addiction.

For me, breast-feeding is perhaps one of the most vital bonding moments between the child and mother. Almost as soon as we are born, our mouth is literally latched onto our mother's breast. Our first oral contact is with her soft nipple, like a celebratory champagne drink ushering us into the world.

The chemical released through the woman's breast milk has been referred to as the "cuddle chemical," since it supports establishing intimacy and trust between the child and mother. It is not surprising to see a newborn drunk upon his or her mother's milk, ready to be bundled up for a peaceful and safe sleep.

It is important to note at this point that I understand some mother's are not able to breast feed their child or do experience a genuine physical separation. This is not to lay blame or impugn their behavior. It's just simply acknowledging that this may have some impact upon the child's emotional development.

Studies have also shown that people who are committed to practicing prayer or meditation experience a similar chemical reaction to that produced by alcohol in the brain. These practices of mindfulness provide opportunities for us to feel the benefits of the cuddle chemical, to bring us back to the sense of mother.

Unfortunately, this beautiful seminal experience of breast-feeding has been tainted for me because it reminds me of how my ex-husband would guzzle down beer. He would lock his fingers onto the bottle, sucking upon it hungrily as would a baby on its mother's teat.

And though he would derive no nutritional benefit, it clearly acted as a nominal substitute, enabling him to abandon himself into a feel-good stupor. Like my ex-husband, most alcoholics build up a tolerance and need to drink copious amounts of alcohol to release the required endorphins to feel happy.

As a mother breast-feeding, I was instantly struck by the same desperate insatiability my children demonstrated while attached to my breast, this one source of nourishment so unique in this world.

In these moments, I knew my children felt seen, held, and heard. From my own instincts as a mother and from what I have observed, this sacred juncture, this correlation between mother and child, is a crucial determinant of how we learn to make ourselves happy.

In Kathleen Gribble's research paper, "Mental Health, Attachment, and Breastfeeding: Implications for Adopted Children and Mothers," she asserts that

> Breastfeeding can play a significant role in developing the attachment relationship between child and mother ... in instances of adoption and particularly where the child has experienced abuse or neglect, the impact of breastfeeding can be considerable.
>
> Breastfeeding may assist attachment development via the provision of regular intimate interaction between mother and child; the calming, relaxing and analgesic impact of breastfeeding on children; and the stress relieving and maternal sensitivity promoting influence of breastfeeding on mothers.
>
> The impact of breastfeeding as observed in cases of adoption has applicability to all breastfeeding

situations, but may be especially relevant to other at risk dyads, such as those families with a history of intergenerational relationship trauma; this deserves further investigation. (2)

(2) Gribble, Karleen. (2006). Mental health, attachment and breastfeeding: Implications for adopted children and their mothers. International breastfeeding journal. 1. 5. 10.1186/1746-4358-1-5.

In both my professional and personal life, I have identified similar links to breast-feeding and later life attachment issues. From this basis, I believe that one could also speculate that some oral addictions related to eating, sucking, smoking, or drinking may be acting as a means of alleviating symptoms related to early childhood issues.

Perhaps you never had the chance to know your mother because she died when you were young. Obviously reasons such as this were not your fault; you were simply born.

In terms of this and other related circumstances, it can be difficult to discover that you are harboring negative emotions or feelings of abandonment toward the very person whom you feel you should have been closest to. But this is okay. It's okay to simply visit these emotions and say, "Hello," to them.

The following tapping scripts are principally targeted at those readers who have made or sense a connection to their addiction in relation to their biological mother. Having said that, some aspects may also relate to a significant mother figure like a grandma, step mom, adopted mother, aunty or sister.

Tapping Script 18

KC   Even though I feel a disconnection from my mother, I love and accept myself.

KC   Even though I didn't always feel safe and protected by my mother, I love and accept myself.

KC   Even though my mother's words and actions may have left me feeling hurt and rejected, I love and accept myself now.

EB   This pain.

SE   These feelings of abandonment.

UE   These feelings of betrayal.

UN   I have sensed them for some time now.

CH   I have felt a deep yearning for my mother.

CB   Perhaps I was not met by my mother as I believed?

UA   My inner child still feels not held by her.

TH   I am thirsty for the love of my mother.

EB   I am thirsty for her encouragement.

SE   I am thirsty for her kindness.

UE   I want to hear her soft tones.

UN   I deserve to hear them.

CH   I want to feel her soft touch.

CB	I deserve her soft touch.
UA	I want to sense her patience and love for me.
TH	I deserved that type of connection as a baby.

EB	I deserve to feel welcomed into the world.
SE	With open arms.
UE	An open heart.
UN	Every baby deserves this.
CH	A happy homecoming.
CB	A celebration.
UA	Warmth and nourishment.
TH	I will start to create a new story.

EB	A story of love.
SE	A story of being wanted.
UE	I will begin with kindness to myself.
UN	What she could not see.
CH	Will now be seen.
CB	What she could not hear.
UA	Will now be heard.
TH	The cries in the night.

EB	Will not be ignored.
SE	The time of real giving.
UE	Will now begin.
UN	This is my promise.
CH	This is my gift to you.
CB	You will be seen.
UA	Beautiful and whole.
TH	Remember, sweet [your name], you are enough.

Remember these emotions are likely to have some factual basis, however deeply buried they are in your psyche. As mentioned, this disconnection may be the result of early abuse or trauma, so it is crucial that they are validated and believed.

The following script is specifically targeted at readers who are already clear that there is a direct link between their attachment issues and their addiction.

<u>Tapping Script 19</u>

KC	Even though my mother could not, would not, take care of me in the way that I needed, I love and accept myself.
KC	Even though I still crave my mother's love, I forgive myself for my needs.
KC	Even though I seek nourishment using [name your addiction], it is safe for me to consider letting it go.

EB	My addiction.
SE	I am an addict.
UE	I am exhausted by my addiction.
UN	So much has been taken from me.
CH	I have lost so much.
CB	I have been in this cycle for too long.
UA	All this denial.
TH	All this stress.

EB	It is time to change.
SE	It is time to let it go.
UE	The child still cries out.
UN	But its cries go unanswered.
CH	My relationship to my mother was hard.
CB	So it is time to move on.
UA	I am not my mother. I am not my addiction.
TH	It is time to let them go.

EB	I must turn up for me now.
SE	I will provide my nourishment.

UE	I will be my shelter.
UN	I am strong enough now.
CH	It is never too late to change.
CB	The world is full of love.
UA	Beyond my mother.
TH	Beyond my addiction.

EB	It is not too late for me to find out.
SE	I can be drug free. I can be sober.
UE	I don't need to hurt myself.
UN	Or those around me anymore.
CH	My addiction cannot help me.
CB	It never really did.
UA	However much I thought it would.
TH	It's time to let it go.

EB	I have been in so much pain.
SE	I have felt so much anger.
UE	I have cried out for help for so long.
UN	Over and over and over.

CH But no one seemed to care. No one ever came.

CB So hear my pain!

UA So hear my anger!

TH It is time for this story to be told.

EB Let it be heard from every cell, from every fiber in my body.

SE I will not be a powerless child anymore.

UE I will not be the victim.

UN I will no longer be kept hostage to my addictions.

CH Because I can nourish myself now.

CB My addiction was never my mother's milk.

UA It was only ever my poison.

TH I will honor my need now.

Stop and breathe. Rest for a moment and reflect on what has surfaced during this tapping.

Exercise

Try to envisage what a warm, nourishing motherly bond might feel like. A good way to go about this is to write an imaginary letter from your mother, expressing love, contrition, and tenderness in order for you to begin a healing process together.

Here is an example I have provided for you.

Dear Child of Mine,

I am so sorry I let you down. I am so sorry that I could not nourish you as you needed. You need to hear me now, that your birth is a gift. You are special beyond belief. You were born perfect and whole, and you still are. You deserve all the love and intimacy a mother and child relationship can give.

Surrender your anger and suffering to me now, child. I am bigger than you. Let me hold your pain now. It is my job to nourish you and protect you. Let me do that. Receive my blessings. Receive my love and pride. I see all the good in you. Let me help you build your confidence. It was my honor to birth you into this world. Live your life with me standing with you and holding your hand. I will not leave you alone. I will wipe away the young child's tears, even those tears that you have shed as an adult.

Believe in your self-worth as I believe in you.

Love, Mum

After you write your own letter, read it out aloud to yourself over and over. Place it on your altar or in a private special place. Begin to feel the separation from the pain and sorrow that should have never been yours and all possibilities beyond it. When you are ready, let your own story of reconciliation begin.

Ritual

Light your candle for your inner child.

Place a cup of milk on your altar.

Greet your inner child with the symbol of mother's milk.

Receive her milk every day at your altar.

Feel the connections to your own healing.

You are loved.

Part 2: To the Addict

To maintain a respectful approach to this topic, I need to acknowledge that many of us have been or are currently battling addiction. I want to say to you emphatically, I know how hard this is. You are no different to the people who have recovered. You are simply at a different stage of healing.

The pain and misery you have endured throughout your life does explain why you have taken this path. You deserve a better quality of life, as do your loved ones. Understand this, that all of our stories are equally valid, unique, and important. As such, I see us as we are, united together in a common bond of abuse and abandonment.

So I say to you, we *will* lift ourselves out of our stories of abuse together.

We must also recognize that the first person one really needs to demonstrate compassion toward is oneself. Only in this way can we truly begin to get in touch with what lies beneath our addiction and create the momentum for real change.

Therefore, it is important to move toward a place of contrition as well as self-forgiveness. In this way, you will be more at ease and ready to express remorse for any damage that you have caused to yourself or others.

We are all generally familiar with the myriad of support services that assist with various drug and alcohol addictions. But the first real step begins within. All it can take is to see and acknowledge that you have been living in a state of disconnection that can often emanate from the mother or mother figure.

A good example of this was while working with a long-term client who originally presented with a condition known as Omphalophobia, whereby she had chronic sensitivity in the navel or the belly button. In some cases, this condition can be brought about by trauma or abuse in this region of the body.

She also confided that she had some issues with how she was managing her alcohol consumption, much like her mother. As these links were made, she became very protective of her mother choosing only to always see her in a positive light. This was the polar opposite for her father whom she considered an abuser who was addicted to marijuana.

"(My father) was like a stalking tiger moving around our tiny lounge room area. No one, not any of us (her siblings) were safe around him. We did not know if he would come at us with his mouth or with his fists. You just never knew with him."

When I asked her where her mother was at these times, she could not provide a definitive answer. When I eluded to the fact that it was part of her mother's job to keep her children safe, she became quite upset and angry.

After long period of absence from our sessions, she returned to counseling with a specific request that we only focus upon the causes of her omphalophobia. Using a tapping script and some hypnotherapy, we began to explore the sources of her phobia. Remarkably she began to struggle to repeat back the tapping script given to her, finally losing the power of speech altogether.

This, we deduced, indicated that her phobia may have began at a preverbal age, when she was a new born. She then told me that her mother suffered from postnatal depression and that she had been handed over to the care of relatives immediately after her birth.

Little is known of what occurred with, or to my client during this three-month period. I then completed another tapping script directed at the abandonment and potential abuse she suffered while away from her mother. She came to accept that she had experienced varying levels of abandonment by her mother, not only to her father's abuse but while she was an infant. Notably, the symptoms of her phobia significantly diminished by the end of this session.

When I met with her next, she reported that her alcohol consumption had greatly reduced. After a great deal of self-reflection and support, she now enjoys a growing sense of self-love and safety in her life. Recently, she proudly announced that she now considers herself a recovering alcoholic who enjoys a much more balanced and nurturing relationship with his mother.

"The long night is over," she tearfully told me.

Obviously, you will need your own particular strategy to progress with your relationship to your mother or mother figure. But, please, do not be too hard on yourself on this new journey of personal growth and learning.

Think of how many times a toddler falls before he or she can even stand up straight, let alone walk. You will fall many times too, and that's okay. Hope will come, and your strength and capacity will grow. Then you will begin to succeed.

Let's do some more tapping in regards to addiction.

Tapping Script 20

KC   Even though addiction has been my main way of coping with my anger and pain, I forgive and accept myself.

KC   Even though I only know my suffering through my addiction, I forgive and accept myself.

KC   Even though I feel a deep sense of shame and anger towards my mother, I love and accept myself for who I am.

EB   This addiction.

SE   It is all mine.

UE   No one can take it from me.

UN   The suffering.

CH   It is in me.

CB   All the time.

UA   I am angry.

TH   And I am expressing my anger through my addiction.

EB   I am feeling rejected.

SE   And I am expressing my rejection through my addiction.

UE   I do feel abandoned.

UN   And I am expressing my abandonment through my addiction.

CB   I cannot give it up.

UA	It is who I am.
TH	It is who I have become.

EB	I have no other way of expressing my pain.
SE	My addiction is my voice.
UE	My addiction is my only way to make a stand.
UN	I don't care what you think.
CB	I am entitled to my addiction.
UA	It belongs to me.
TH	You can't take it away from me.

EB	All this anger.
SE	All this responsibility to get sober.
UE	I don't want it.
UN	I am the victim here.
CH	When I am drunk/high/stoned.
CB	I feel hungry for love.
UA	I feel hungry for attention.
TH	I feel overwhelmed.

EB	I admit I am tired of this way of coping.
SE	I am locked into it, and I have no way out.
UE	Okay, I admit it now, I need help.
UN	It's time to make a change.
CH	There is no shame in it.
CB	So I call on hope.
UA	Because I really want to know.
TH	What's on the other side of my addiction?

EB	On the other side.
SE	There are those who live without it.
UE	There are those who have made a stand.
UN	Why can't I?
CH	I know I can stick to it.
UA	But I know I will sometimes fall.
TH	I know I will sometimes fail.

EB	I have had enough of going backwards.
SE	I want to go forward.
UE	There are other places to be.

UN	There are other places to go.
CH	I can feel love when I am drunk/high/stoned.
CB	But now I want to reach real happiness.
UA	And not an artificial high.
TH	I want to feel like I am really there!

Well done. Take a moment and feel the possibility of change.

Exercise

I want you to look back over your life and think of the people you have hurt: family, friends, or acquaintances. Write down their names, and start a letter of apology. You do not need to send it to them; just write it all down as if you were going to. If you are able, tell them how sorry you are.

Describe the event or situation where you let them down. Look through their eyes as the event or situation unfolded. Feel and name the hurt that you perceived they felt. Try to express the grace and compassion that they deserved in your letter. Name your own personal regrets and reflections. Perhaps you can also write down how you were suffering a deep hurt or were subjected to abuse that motivated your actions.

Take your time.

Feel the deep connection to each person (whether the person is alive or deceased). Now read aloud each letter, and tap using the following script. Imagine the person standing in the room, receiving your words of apology. Remember, this is a powerful step toward taking responsibility for your addiction and its effects on others.

Time for some tapping

Tapping Script 21

KC   Even though I have hurt all these people in my life, I am willing to consider forgiving myself.

KC   Even though I have abandoned and rejected [name person], I love, honor, and accept all the people I have named.

KC   Even though some of my actions have been abusive toward [name person], I am beginning the healing process.

EB   All of my toxic behavior.

SE   So many memories of hurting others.

UE   What was I thinking?

UN   I wasn't thinking straight.

CH   At times, I was out of control.

CB   This addiction was like an infection that I shared with others.

UA   I have shared it with so many people.

TH   I am so sorry.

EB   I am so sorry I broke your trust, [name person].

SE   I am so sorry I abandoned you when you needed me most.

UE   But it is time I forgave myself.

UN   It is time I ask for your forgiveness.

CH   Please forgive me, [name person].

CB	I have hated myself for so long.
UA	But now I must make room for grace.
TH	I see how I have hurt you, [name person].
EB	I see the damage.
SE	I will make room for you now.
UE	Room for us both.
UN	I hear you.
CH	We can heal together.
CB	We will heal together.
UA	You matter to me, [name person].
TH	I am sorry for all the pain I caused you.
EB	I make a commitment to heal.
SE	*I am* making a commitment to change.
UE	You matter so much to me.
UN	You matter more than my addictions.
CH	You matter more than my abuse.
CB	You matter more than my past.
UA	May there be peace between us.
TH	May it begin to grow.

Well done. Use this script as many times as you need to, until the sense of saying sorry is fully realized in your heart.

Part 3: Living with the Addict

Observing my ex-husband in the throes of his alcoholic binges could be a daunting yet powerful experience. He was well practiced in the strategy of deeply suppressing his emotions, so much so that it became part of his identity, how he understood the world and his place within it.

His suffering, real or perceived, created a kind of dispensation when it came to his addiction. His abandonment to it necessitated that others around him become entangled in his *special* need.

The worst expression of this came when he physically grabbed me and pushed me against a wall, believing that I had sent someone to kill him. He had been drinking heavily all day and had entered a paranoid delusional state. To this day, I still shiver as I recall his scowling beer-stinking mouth nearly touching mine, while he screamed at me like a madman.

In this, and in many other situations, his personal regard for me or our children in the home was simply nonexistent. Later, he would try to rectify this situation through therapy. But he was doomed to fail, as his feelings and thoughts came from a place of pain that no one was ever allowed to reach.

Notably, his own mother could not tolerate his drinking; however, this did not stop him. Looking through the lens of his disconnected childhood, I came to see that his drinking allowed him to regress back into an infantile state, enabling him to rekindle all the old negative attention-seeking patterns of his childhood, such as tantrums and other impulsive behaviors.

A clear example of this was when he was prevented from meeting a drinking buddy because we had an important commitment to visit family and friends. On this particular occasion, I can remember him raging at me in public, as if I had taken something precious from him. This, along with a number of other episodes, highlighted the value he placed upon his freedom to consume alcohol, as if it was almost a sacred act to him.

I believe these kinds of responses gave him the opportunity to recapture the kind of turbulent relationship he had shared with his mother, thus giving him a pathway back to what was familiar and understandable in his life.

I believe these entrenched behaviors reflected a deep-seated anger, an unexpressed resentment directed particularly toward his mother. All this led to a toxic trail of antisocial behavior and abusive traits, which invariably took control of his life. He created an energy around himself, like a violent storm, crashing indiscriminately through the collective psyche of everyone around him, sparing no one in its wake.

Eventually, there was no safe place to be, no safe place to go. Socializing became a quagmire of embarrassing gaffes, humiliating moodiness, or just outright bursts of aggression. Memories, promises, and priorities were constantly lost or forgotten, so much so that any variation from the dictates of his distorted version of events was attacked or ridiculed.

From my own observations, many addicts become almost possessed by a chemically induced sense of entitlement, a kind of artificial grandiosity, whereby the needs of others are always secondary, sometimes losing their relevancy altogether. The family and those closest to the addict become collateral damage, caught up in their own inner turmoil.

In my ex-husband's case, he would threaten to take away our children if the true nature of his addiction was ever revealed in public. This reinforced my powerlessness, locking me back into a script of silence, as had been the case with my cousin and father.

Once again, I was with a man who was more concerned for his own protection than mine. Eventually, his brokenness made me feel trapped and alone in his unmet, unquenchable needs.

In many ways, addiction remains a taboo or hidden point of discussion in society, reinforcing the silence that keeps so many of us trapped in the addict's cycles of abuse. What's more, the behavior may eventually ensnare the nonaddict, leading to addictions and other mental health issues of their own.

For me, living with the addict meant nothing was spared, not our family, not our home, not our marriage, not even my integrity as a human being.

So many of us dutifully tolerate these addictions in our relationships. We feel we are bound to our marital commitments, our need for financial safety, and the hope that they can somehow "turn things around." There are other times, between the madness, when we can see hope and the possibility of a new, healthy relationship.

But invariably, abuse and abandonment are lurking just around the corner, ready to pounce, and so we continuously feel duped and frustrated by their inadequacies, repeating the same conversation over and over again. Eventually, we come to the terrible conclusion that all hope is lost, and we must simply let go.

Let's do some tapping to heal.

Tapping Script 22

KC   Even though I am carrying trauma in my body, I love and accept myself.

KC   Even though I was so overwhelmed in my relationship to [name addict], I love and forgive myself.

KC   Even though I feel sorry and sad, I love and forgive myself for feeling powerlessness.

EB   All this fear.

SE   Still in my body.

UE   All this terror.

UN   Still in my body.

CH   All this sadness.

CB   Still in my body.

UA   All these feelings.

TH   Still in my body.

EB   I really didn't feel safe with [name addict].

SE   I still don't feel safe with him/her.

UE   I am just honoring that.

UN   I really had no control over his or her actions.

CH   [Name addict] really had no control over his or her actions.

CB	He or she didn't try to stop.
UA	He or she should have stopped.
TH	But now all I want is to understand why.

EB	[Name addict] put me in danger.
SE	Mentally and physically.
UE	[Name addict] was only concerned about themself.
UN	I am releasing myself from all that now.
CH	I am releasing myself from his or her hold.
CB	I deserve safe and loving relationships.
UA	I deserve this above all things.
TH	There is no going back.

EB	So, I forgive myself for hanging in there.
SE	I forgive myself for placing myself second.
UE	I forgive myself for giving power over to [name addict].
UN	I forgive myself for putting those I love in harm's way.
CH	I forgive myself for not asking for more.
CB	Even though I was doing my best.

UA	It was not enough to keep me safe.
TH	It was never going to be enough.

EB	I know this now.
SE	So I will ask for help.
UE	There is no shame in it.
UN	By putting myself first.
CH	I'm learning I have a choice.
CB	Even when I didn't.
UA	And for that I am sad.
TH	But I have endured, so it is time to acknowledge *me*.

EB	I give myself permission to acknowledge myself.
SE	I give myself permission to acknowledge my life.
UE	I give myself permission to acknowledge my work.
UN	I give myself permission to acknowledge my victories.
CH	I give myself permission to acknowledge my lessons learned.
CB	I give myself permission to acknowledge my changes.
UA	I give myself permission to acknowledge my future.
TH	And all I can be.

Continue to tap until some of the old pain and hurt leaves your body.

I did recognize that my ex-husband needed help, but my actions of attending to his needs and compensating for him only put off the inevitable. In the end, like a first responder in a medical crisis, I ascertained that I needed to keep myself and my children safe before I could hope to "save" him.

Just making these kinds of personal reflections is extraordinary. For me, it gave perspective on the true nature of the situation and the need to begin envisaging what life would be like, beyond the addiction of my ex-husband.

So there came a time when I decided I was no longer prepared to live with someone not willing to face his addiction. I finally mustered the courage to take this step to reclaiming my own personal power and, in doing so, rediscovered something beautiful and lost for so long: my own inner child.

As I outlined earlier in this book, the simple rituals of honoring my inner child helped me pave the way to saying no to my ex-husband's abuse. Therefore, I would no longer tolerate living with him if he did not deal with his alcoholism. And since his addiction and sense of self were so intertwined, he effectively made the decision for me to leave him.

Though the decision to go was incredibly painful, I do not have any long-term regrets. He still remains embroiled in his alcoholism, so for me, I made the right choice. I hope you are able to make the right choice, whether or not you remain in your relationship.

Exercise

Do you have a similar story to tell? What has your life been like to date? What comparisons can you draw in your own story while dealing with the addicted? Were they angry, withdrawn, violent, abandoning, or perhaps depressive? Who protected you? Who was meant to protect you? Were you often left alone? Did anyone provide you with emotional support or counseling? What stops you from saying no more? What is keeping you in the relationship?

Write down your responses.

Let's do some tapping.

Tapping Script 23

KC   Even though I have had no control over [name the person], I love and accept myself.

KC   Even though I have been repeatedly hurt by [name the person], I love and accept who I am.

KC   Even though I have felt so lost and overwhelmed living with [name the person], I love myself.

EB   All this abuse.

SE   All the hypocrisy.

UE   All the lies.

UN   All the broken promises.

CH   All the fears.

CB   All the loneliness.

UA   All my life.

TH   When will it stop?

EB	I feel trapped.
SE	Trapped like a victim.
UE	I am trapped.
UN	What power do I have to create change?
CH	If I cannot change.
CB	What hope is there for me?
UA	It is the same question over and over.
TH	The same answer.

EB	So many broken promises.
SE	So many second chances.
UE	All this sadness.
UN	It repeats itself.
CH	Over and over again.
CB	When will it stop?
UA	I need it to stop.
TH	I need [name addict] to stop.

EB	I rely on [name addict] income.
SE	I rely on [name addict] companionship.

UE	I am afraid to let go of this relationship.
UN	Who am I without [name addict]?
CH	Who am I without this drama?
CB	Feeling like a victim is familiar to me.
UA	I am ashamed to admit this.
TH	I'm tired of filling in all the gaps.

EB	I take on more responsibility than I should.
SE	I'm not the addict; [name addict] is.
UE	I will take back my power.
UN	Because I am not the addict.
CH	I can create change.
CB	Even if [name addict] cannot.
UA	I will create safety.
TH	Even if [name addict] cannot.

EB	Even though I have lost hope that [name addict] can change.
SE	This doesn't mean that I can't.
UE	I want to change.
UN	I *will* change!

CH   It is safe for me to do so.

CB   I allow this for myself.

UA   I *will* take control.

TH   I am not a child anymore.

As we discovered in chapter 5, *no* is a powerful little word. Like a small shift in a rudder, saying this word can begin a journey far away from where we expected to end up.

Using the very short tapping script that follows, repeat it over and over again with a growing sense of authority. If you wish, name all the things that you want to be free of, in relation to addiction.

Tapping Script 24

EB   I will rise.

SE   Above you.

UE   Above myself.

UN   Above it all.

CH   No more, I say.

CB   No more.

UA   No! No! No! No! No! No! No!

TH   Even if [name addict] won't change, I will.

Let go of all the secrets you kept to protect the addict. Release the old wounds that keep you feeling powerless. Whatever you decide, wherever this journey now takes you, remember the safety of yourself and those you care for, is paramount.

Ritual

> Light your candle.
>
> Tell your inner child.
>
> Yes to boundaries.
>
> Yes to empowerment.
>
> Yes to love.
>
> No to the pain.
>
> No to the resentment.
>
> No to the lies.
>
> Yes to me.
>
> Yes to you.
>
> We are safe now.

CHAPTER 11
MATCH STICK GIRL

GROWING UP IN a working-class suburb generally meant money was scarce. Coming from a family of eight siblings, I mainly wore second- or even third-hand clothes during most of my younger years. It was not until my early teens that I finally began to wear newly purchased clothing. I still remember my first pair of denim jeans because I never took them off. Such was my sense of pride.

My account of my childhood money story is by no means special. In fact, it is a common one experienced by many people of my generation. However, it is important to establish a clear link in respect to how money is used as a source of power, in relation to my upbringing.

It is also essential to point out that I have no sense of social stigma in relation to my family's modest economic circumstances. I appreciate that my father did his best, considering his level of schooling. In fact, his ability to self-educate had always remained a point of inspiration for me and my siblings.

What I did find extremely challenging was the draconian manner in which he ruled over the family finances, ultimately shaping my personal relationship to money. I learned from a very early age that men, like my father, controlled it, and women, like me, were given restricted access.

From the get-go, I came to understand that men are the breadwinners and that women waited to receive the money. Though my mother principally managed the household expenditures, she got what she was given like the rest of us, with no real say in the matter.

I have reoccurring memories, where I was terrified of my father whenever I dared asked for some money. Coupled with this terror was a stinging shame when the inevitable answer was "No!" As a result, I have come to see how shame and terror informed my ongoing money choices, making me feel unworthy to even have an expectation of financial success or abundance.

As a young teenager, I aligned with my mother's money story. I was socially predestined to be the good Catholic housewife, with little thought of a professional career. Subsequently, I came to believe and expect a man would step in and take on his rightful role of controlling my finances.

I did work in my twenties but never had enough money or management skills to fully realize its potential. Although I was accepted into university, I decided to go into the workforce, which my father had insisted upon. It was as if he had somehow decided that I did not have the aptitude to seek higher education. In fact, I always felt I was considered the stupid one of the family.

This perspective was further reinforced by his reaction when I told him that I had passed my high school final exams with flying colors. All he could muster was a muted, "Oh."

I was hurt by this, as he was unable to share my first great crowning moment in life, as a young adult, unable to give me the parental approval I so dearly craved from him. The fact that my father still cannot acknowledge my wisdom and intelligence remains a painful open wound that may never completely heal.

After a three-year stint in the public service, I found myself bored and unsatisfied, but I had successfully developed the capacity to better save my own money. It was at this time I began to dream of finally taking up my university placement in order to qualify as a schoolteacher.

I had an enduring vision of working with young children and helping them build their sense of self-esteem—something that I believed was sorely missing from the school curriculum at the time. However, to be safe, I ensured that I was given a nine-month sabbatical from my current employment in the public service.

When I commenced my further education, I was one of fifty entrants out of five hundred applicants. This made me feel incredibly proud of myself, since I felt I was among an elite few. Moreover, my own personal vision, my own sense of self, was finally coming into being, but my rejoicing was short-lived, as my father was furious at me for having left my paid position, albeit on leave.

My father's wrath was an economic one. I was expected to pay the same amount of board despite no longer earning my full-time income. In fact, he did not speak to me for weeks, so angered was he that I would dare to waver from the path he had chosen for me. I still remember the pain associated with his stony silence. And despite the past abuse I had sustained, I still wanted to impress him.

What's more, my parents no longer faced the same economic struggles of my childhood. This was evident in the fact they had had several holidays abroad and were on a much higher income, with only two of my siblings still at home. The simple fact of the matter was he did not need the money. He simply wanted to punish me and keep me small and oppressed, seeking his pound of flesh even at the cost of our relationship.

I felt alone, and once again, my mother did not stand by me. I went to university with my father's anger and contempt hanging over me every day I attended. I paid the money as asked, submitting to his authority.

But I was still only twenty-one with relatively little experience of the world beyond his control. In hindsight, I have come to understand the intrinsic logic of his cruelty, which I believe emanated from his own patriarchal upbringing. He too was prevented from higher education and sent off to work, in order to fill his dying father's shoes.

Yet this abuse was twofold. I had already endured his sexual abuse as a young girl, and now, here again, I was emotionally broken by the use of money as a weapon to assert his control. Notably at no time did he ever ask me what I wanted from my life, since my input into such matters seemed null and void. I believe he perceived it as wrong to give a woman too much economic freedom, perhaps because it would cause her to become wayward, maybe even a threat to his power.

As such, I was parented by my father as if he owned me. In such circumstances, there was no real understanding, no way of knowing what it meant to nourish me spiritually or encourage my authentic voice. He was the first of so many men who could not see me as I truly wanted to be. He was the first to take and not give back.

Eventually, it became apparent that I had to finally escape my father's control if I were to attain any sense of identity. This meant I needed to move out of the home. Unfortunately, my savings from work had dwindled away, leaving me ill equipped to cope with independent living.

Subsequently, I only did a year of my degree. I simply didn't have the skill set or confidence to break through my father's disappointment in me. The motivation and vision to achieve the teaching diploma was worn down by my own preconditioning.

That familiar voice, the inner critic kept telling me, "How could I have even thought I could take back control for myself, to take it from my father?"

It was if I had a foreign spy in my own mind, seeking to control and frustrate my efforts for self-determination, maintaining a destructive allegiance to my father's beliefs.

At the end of the day, all I really wanted to do was avoid the callousness I had experienced in my childhood, which had now re-emerged in my money story with my father. It seemed that it was my destiny to remain seated, numb, and abandoned, in his lap, just like it once was, just like that little girl.

And so, I dutifully went back to full-time work, fully convincing myself I had attained some level of self-direction and purpose. The awful truth of the matter was I was still operating in accordance with my father's expectations.

Exercise

Write down your own personal history in terms of money. Reflect upon the way it has shaped your life choices, particularly in respect to your personal relationships.

Consider the following:

- *How have you accessed money in your life—through working, spouses, your family, as well as other relationships?*
- *What level of control did you have over its distribution?*
- *What has been the amount you have been able to retain?*
- *Has it reflected your true worth?*
- *What has been your life role in relation to it—caregiver, breadwinner? Has it been an empowering or disempowering experience for you?*
- *How has money impacted upon your relationships in the past and the present?*
- *What do you consider to be your own value in terms of money? Is it a friend or the enemy?*
- *Where have these money choices taken you in life?*
- *Consider how they have impacted upon your sense of identity: good and bad?*
- *What would you have changed?*
- *What can you change now?*
- *Are you avoiding making the necessary life changes?*
- *Why is this so?*

Time to tap.

Tapping Script 25

KC   Even though I feel lost in my money story, I love and accept myself.

KC   Even though I have felt shame in my money story, I love and accept myself.

KC   Even though I have surrendered control of my finances to others, I love and forgive myself.

EB   I'm afraid to take financial responsibility.

SE   Because I have never done it before.

UE   Because I never thought I needed to.

UE   It was just how I was brought up.

UN   To let [name the abuser/controller] take control.

CH   I did not want his or her anger.

CB   I do not want to be abandoned by him or her.

UA   But these are old ways, old rules.

TH   That have no place in my life now.

EB   I am so tired.

SE   I am sick of being scared.

UE   I am sick of just the crumbs.

UN   I need to take something back for me.

CH	And for those I love.
CB	I will act from a place of prosperity.
UA	I will not take from others, as others took from me.
TH	I am tired of being dominated and owned.
EB	I want my own money now.
SE	I am a giving person.
UE	And I want to give more.
UN	I want to stand alone in my own money story.
CH	I have a right to be as big as I want to be.
CB	I have a right to be safe to earn all the money I can.
UA	It is safe to let go of the past.
TH	That old money story is going.
EB	It is safe for me to ask for what I want.
SE	It is safe for me to say hello to money.
UE	I can be friends with it now.
UN	I can share in its abundance.
CH	I release myself from my prison of impoverishment.
CB	That turned me into a prisoner of my upbringing.

UA   That turned me into a prisoner of society.

TH   That turned me into a prisoner of [name the abuser / controller's] beliefs.

My parents left me believing I needed to be married in order to gain access to money. In this way, I would truly be an upright woman in their eyes. But the lie would eventually come crashing down around me, when it became clear that my husband could no longer control his alcoholism and abuse. What I didn't realize, what I couldn't understand at the time, was that I had been set up to fail and that the seeds of my financial sabotaging would only be fully realized when I left my marriage.

The divorce came at a high cost. I was left living below the poverty line with three very young boys. What money I had in my own right would soon dwindle away, as it had done under my father's rule while at university. Like my father, my ex-husband financially punished me for deciding upon a different direction to my life. This would find full expression when I was left to fend completely for our sons after he became unemployed.

He has since remained prosperous, having received a large family inheritance, none of which has been put toward the immediate upkeep of our children. Consequently, I had become poorer while he has become richer.

At this point in my life, I simply needed money to raise my children. By anyone's standards, this was more than an adequate reason to desire money in greater abundance. A deep sense of dread ensued, as I contemplated the prospect of having no money, no house, and no food. I even began to question my capabilities as a mother. My inner critic gave me no quarter, mocking me at every chance.

"See! See what happens when you leave your man! You can't handle this! You are just a woman, just a mother, and you can't even get that right!"

So this seemed to be my punishment. For making a stand to protect myself and my children, I was condemned to a life heading toward poverty.

I was literally on my knees, falling apart. Great bouts of sobbing did little to nullify the shame and fear surging through my body. I felt like I was walking through life on a tightrope with my safety net of savings left in tatters.

Hope had become a distant memory. In large part, I had convinced myself I was just living out the consequences of my predetermined life. This ominous insight inspired me to seek ways to create a new money story that would lead to greater financial prosperity. Eventually, this came in the form of an ever-increasing client load in my therapy practice.

However, my opportunity to act upon this growing prosperity was snatched away from me as a result of my sons becoming completely estranged from their father. This required me to take them on full-time. So once again, emotional abuse and neglect by my ex-husband had found its way back to me, this time through my children.

As the contact with their father ceased, so did the trickle of financial support he was giving me. Now I was a full-time single mother, which completely overwhelmed me. In my stressed and deluded state, I convinced myself that my ex-husband's failure, as both a caregiver and a breadwinner, was somehow a shameful testimony to my own inability to find a suitable partner to support myself and my children.

My mental health was greatly impacted, resulting in an inability to adequately nourish and support my clients. Subsequently, client numbers declined, further adding to my financial woes. Money, became a fair-weather friend, that stopped knocking on my door. It truly felt like the universe itself was conspiring against me.

When I reflect upon my state of mind at the time, it reminds me of the story of "The Matchstick Girl." It's New Year's Eve, and the

Matchstick Girl is trying to sell her matches, barefoot and shivering in the snow. She peers through a window at a loving, warm, and prosperous family enjoying their feast. But no such joy was to be had for the Matchstick Girl at her home. Instead, she had only an angry father waiting to beat her if she did not return with coin in exchange for the matches.

Having sold no matches but too afraid to return home, she lights them to stay warm. She begins to have visions of a roast duck dinner, a Christmas tree, and a hot stove. Eventually, the matches are all used up, and she dies alone and uncared for in the snow.

I was that little Matchstick Girl, spiritually frozen and impoverished, with a father who had only cared about what he could take from her. Like this girl burning up her matches, I was burning through my savings with visions of those things that would never be mine. Eventually, I too would be "dead" financially.

Something had to give.

It was then that I heard with clarity the kind yet directive inner voice, that told me "Go learn about money." It was the same voice that had told me not to close the door in my apartment during my asthma attack.

The solution seemed simple enough, and I had the perfect tool to begin this process: the emotional freedom technique. I began to tap in earnest with fresh new insights emerging almost daily, one of the first being that if I remained small, I would be less of a target for my father and my ex-husband's retribution and thus avoid being abused or abandoned by them.

As absurd as all this sounds, my primitive brain still took a lot of coaxing to get it past this very irrational way of thinking. This realization also highlighted to me how powerful my basic fight-flight-freeze responses were and how much they still affected my overall outlook on life.

Also, as instructed by the voice, I enrolled myself in Nick Ortner's online course, "The Tapping Solution for Financial Abundance". This was a game-changer for me. I now had a practical step-by-step approach to guide me through my financial issues and each and every underlying belief that had created my initial dysfunction.

However, there were still some very nasty surprises in store for me as I challenged this old thinking, ready to rear up at me from my subconscious.

The night before I started the online course, I had a dream. I am in my bedroom asleep. I wake up to a noise. I look outside and see several men are approaching the front door. I am terrified. I check that the door is locked. Yet, to my horror, the men open the door as if no lock exists. I run to a window to escape in fear of being raped or killed. I just manage to get away, fleeing to the protection of my neighbors.

I woke up absolutely petrified. I now realized that the echoes of my father's beliefs still reverberated strongly in my subconscious. The old memories from my childhood were warning me not to seek a pathway toward my own money. And even though I had not lived with the man for thirty-two years, he was still sending these men to scare me back into submission.

As the meaning of this nightmare unfolded, I tried to raise my hand to tap. But could only manage to move one finger to tap on one point. However, I slowly regained my strength, and a new force arose in my body, releasing me from my fear.

As I tapped, I realized that my neighbors represented the protection I would be afforded as I sought out the means to find financial independence. After that, I voraciously consumed each of Ortner's online webinars, while meticulously keeping a journal, noting down all my reflections and memories in relation to any money matters.

Each webinar gave me an insight into other people's money stories. These shared episodes of shame, anger, and guilt helped me realize

I was not alone. It also helped me come to terms with my current financial circumstances and believe that I could truly guide myself to a sustainable level of ongoing prosperity.

Okay, let's tap now.

Tapping Script 26

KC   Even though I have been trapped in my own money story, I love and accept who I am.

KC   Even though [name abuser/controller) treated me like he or she owned me, I love and accept who I am.

KC   Even though I have felt frightened and frozen in both body and spirit, I love and accept myself.

EB   It is safe for me to release this fear.

SE   This terror.

UE   From all the cells of my body.

UN   From all the cells of my body.

CH   All this shock in my body.

CB   It has been frozen in there, for such a long time.

UA   All this shock in my body.

TH   All this shock and fear in my body.

EB	It is safe to name it for what it is.
SE	Shame and fear.
UE	Shame and fear.
UN	Shame and fear.
CH	I release you both from my body.
CB	I release you both to the light.
UA	In your place, there will be hope.
TH	In your place, there will be prosperity.

EB	In your place, there will be abundance.
SE	I want to share what I have.
UE	I want to share it all.
UN	I am asking for more now.
CH	Enough is enough.
CB	It's okay to ask.
UA	To give and be given to.
TH	There is enough to go around.

EB	So I will rise.
SE	I will rise now.

UE   This is the time.

UN   There will be no other.

CH   Because I am in charge of my money story.

CB   I see clearly now.

UA   I deserve more.

TH   *I am* deserving.

Whether you consider it the work of God or me triggering a series of positive circumstances based upon my new outlook on life, I found myself paying back old credit card debts and actually moving into a position of saving money. I even created a vision board so that my earning goals were now visible. A once impossible way of living was now opening up before my eyes!

What's more, new opportunities were emerging from unexpected sources. I received a reply from a job interview that had occurred eighteen months earlier. Out of the blue, I was asked to start work within the week. Simultaneously, my private practice also began to thrive. Between the new job and my practice, I was finally on the road to being a financial success. Hallelujah!

Another example was the support I was given for my youngest son, who was experiencing isolation issues, after most of his primary school friendship group started attending a local private high school. I tapped upon this issue, eventually summoning the courage to contact the school about its fee structure.

So moved were they by my story, they decided to offer my son a place at a substantially reduced fee level. In addition to this, a very dear friend and several others helped foot the bill for the school fees. I realized in all of this that I was not only changing my own money story, but I was changing that of my son's.

Finally, through the kindness of friends and strangers, I did not need to view myself through the critical lens of condemnation and shame. Finally, I had begun to walk away from the edge of my financial abyss.

At times, I again remember the old Matchstick Girl story, and I found it interesting how much my own personal perspective had changed toward this story in only a matter of months.

I remember thinking, when I decided to take control of my own money story, *You know what, Brigit? To hell with dying alone and scared in the street. I'm going to keep my own damn matches and make my own damn money for myself and for those I truly love!*

But life is no fairy tale. At the time, I texted my family, letting them know how excited and proud I was for getting on top of my money situation. I also took this as an opportunity to thank them all for their financial support they had given my sons and myself over the years. However, I did not receive one reply from any of my eight siblings!

Momentarily, I felt my personal pride shrink away. However, it then occurred to me that they were the product of the same money story. Subsequently, the scope of our money success had been collectively shaped by our father. And so for me, to step outside this financial pecking order, meant that I was likely to provoke a sense of indifference or perhaps ill ease among my siblings.

In the end, this episode only reinforced my desire to no longer live under the shadow of my upbringing. I would emerge as a truly strong woman in my own right. I am, in fact, thankful for this wall of silence, as I was able to crash through the glass ceiling, setting my own financial compass in the direction I wanted to take.

Okay, let's get back to changing the wiring in our money brains. Use this next script to specifically target past hidden fears you may have had about money. Remember, much can emerge as you move through the tapping exercises, including deep-seated regrets, fears, anxieties, and so on.

Tapping Script 27

KC   Even though I think people want to keep me small and unseen, I love and accept who I am.

KC   Even though I am ashamed of my money situation, I love and forgive myself.

KC   Even though I have played a part in sabotaging my own financial success, I understand I was just trying to stay safe.

EB   All that sabotaging.

SE   All those unsaved dollars.

UE   All those financial failures.

UN   I forgive myself now.

CH   How many times did I tell myself, "What's the point? I give up."

CB   I understand now I was just trying.

UA   To not rock the boat.

TH   To stay safe in my money story.

EB   The only one I have known.

SE   The one they let me have.

UE   I thought I was too lazy.

UN   I thought I was too dumb.

UN   I thought I was too ill equipped.

CH	I thought I had no business in having more money.
CB	I thought I had no right.
UA	I'm choosing to overcome this problem now.
TH	It is my job to support me.

EB	It is my time.
SE	It is my time to act.
UE	I want to be successful.
UN	And I want to show everybody I am worthy of this challenge.
CH	Because I am worthy.
CB	I am worthy of more money.
UA	It will come to me.
TH	And I will freely say hello to it as it arrives.

EB	I no longer want to be safe and small.
SE	I want to step up and be big.
UE	I want to feel safe in my money story now.
UN	I want to feel calm in my money story now.
CH	I want to feel relaxed in my money story now.
CB	Only then will my abundance grow.

UA   I can do this.

TH   I have got this.

If your money story is similar to mine, you can choose to move beyond the choices that have been made in the past.

But you must act.

For the sake of yourself and those who depend upon you financially, you must rise. Rise above the old restraints and the old rules. See this as a way into your own self-directed decision making, which will allow you to generate the necessary personal capital you need.

I know of a number of situations whereby people improved their financial circumstances, moving beyond the psychological entrapments that kept them small and weak. Many came to view their situation as an adventure or a worthy challenge to overcome, rather a personal indictment.

In many of these cases, EFT proved to be a useful tool to help them bring clarity, healing, and abundance. So I ask that you call upon what is great in you. If you act upon such matters from a position of altruism and kindness, you are more likely to manifest what is needed in your life. Often, it will emanate from untapped sources. So take back control of what is rightfully yours.

By the way, if this topic is of specific interest to you, I suggest some experts on this subject, such as Margaret Lynch (*Tapping into Wealth*) and Nick Ortner (*The Tapping Solution*). Both have great insights in relation to money matters.

Ritual

Light your candle for your inner child.

Leave a gold coin on the altar.

Abundance is at hand.

And the child shall be nourished.

CHAPTER 12
LEAVING MY FATHER'S LAP

BEING IN LOVE is one of the most significant life experiences I have ever had. To feel that elemental impulse, the mystical spark, those first intimate, amorous words is a sensation that can momentarily transcend all other desires and wants, a blueprint of sorts that can make or break our future relationships, a thing to die for.

Such was the case with Shakespeare's *Romeo and Juliet*. This concept of love was exquisitely simple: "I cannot live without this other person." Their age-old story demonstrates the drama of love that can befall us all. Whatever our age or circumstances, we can all aspire toward this level of bonding. For many of us, it becomes a lifelong obsession, to find or recapture those first throes of passion that ignited our original notion of *true* love.

Over time, however, this concept of love can get worn down. For many of us, it sets up an inevitable conflict between "How much can I love?" and "How much will it cost me?" This for me is best epitomized by Romeo and Juliet's warring families: the Capulets and Montagues. Both families become so fearful of being hurt or humiliated by Romeo and Juliet's love that they are prepared to crush it—and each other. We too can end up wanting to eliminate the threat of love by setting impossible benchmarks, which drift ever higher with each romantic disappointment.

I often hear my married clients bemoaning the fact that their wife or husband is not living up to their notions of true love. Sometimes, their partner has engaged in some kind of infidelity or taken liberties that only reinforce their feelings of anger and contempt. This can lead into cycles of despair and feelings of abandonment. Despite all the sacrifices made, all the humiliations tolerated, ultimately some couples are so embittered that the possibilities of rekindling any kind of affection are remote.

At the heart of all this misery is the belief that our partner simply doesn't make us happy anymore. But a fair question to ask oneself is "Was it ever his or her job in the first place?" Are we, in fact, languishing in our unmet hopes, expectations, and desires, as well as the need to quench our own loneliness?

Exercise

It is perhaps timely at this point to ask yourself some of the following questions:

- *Why does love have to be so complicated, when it can start off so easily?*
- *What kind of feelings has it created in you, both positive and negative?*
- *How much time and energy have you given to love?*
- *How have you felt during and after the relationship?*
- *What kinds of expectations have you placed upon previous lovers? Were they realistic upon reflection?*
- *Consider what you have lost to your relationship(s)—for example, financial power, possession of your body, trust, identity, friendship, or your own mental and physical health?*
- *Is it possible to rekindle your relationship despite all these hardships? What will you do if you cannot reconnect?*

Despite centuries of social advancement, we are still bombarded by simplistic "happily ever after" notions of a true love, sustained principally through fairy tales, love songs, reality TV, the internet, and so on.

It is of little wonder that we try to protect ourselves from these delusions of love by creating readymade excuses to compensate for the inevitable failure of our relationships. We become so committed to this course of action that we are prepared to go to our graves knowing that our idea of love may have never been met, but at least it remained unchallenged.

As survivors of abuse, this issue can be further complicated for us, as our ideas about love can be quite different from traditional societal perceptions. For me, love found its origins in the lap of my father. These experiences directly influenced my selection of future partners, as I was automated to accept that my needs would always be secondary to their sexual wants and desires.

We need to accept that the very wiring in our brains may have been altered as a result of abuse, especially if it occurred when were very young. In that sense, it is ludicrous to believe that we can just act normal, since normal was made alien to us. For many, our accepted way of acting, of being, may be foreign or even mystifying to others.

Generally speaking, central to any notions of love is trust. To trust someone requires a feeling of confidence and security with another person. We humans assume that the trust will be met by our parents or significant others. As such, we are essentially programmed to surrender our trust to them.

So when trust has been broken down in these circumstances, it follows that we can develop an inability to form natural, healthy connections. Therefore, we are less likely to feel relaxed, hopeful, and self-assured.

A person who has experienced abuse and abandonment has much to consider when allowing a relationship into his or her life. He or she may become preoccupied trying to uncover false promises, bare-face lies, or veiled threats he or she associated with their abuser, all of which creates an understandable level of suspicion and concern.

Over time, our own self-sabotaging mind may ensnare us in never-ending patterns of distrust and betrayal, until we see every relationship through the eyes of our frightened, abused child self. We can also find ourselves feeling abandoned by a poor decision or choice made by our partner. However, we experience it at catastrophic levels, creating a situation where we fight or even break up, though we never began with that intention.

These monsters we foist upon our partners can be a reflection of our own jaded past, having lost sight of the fact that our partner can make mistakes, just like anyone else, while dealing with their own array of shortcomings and emotional fault lines.

We become forever vigilant, sizing up every flaw, every utterance, every sigh, until the initial magic of our relationship is gone, leaving in its wake the haunted past deeds of our abusers.

There is a wonderful fable in the book *Leaving My Father's House* by Marion Woodman. It tells the story of a young princess called Allerleirauh. Whilst on her deathbed, her mother makes her father, the king, vow to never remarry anyone who did not match her renowned beauty.

However, despite all his efforts, the king is unable to find a suitable match. As Allerleirauh matures, she turns into the spitting image of her mother. In a desperate act to honor his promise, the king compels his daughter to marry him, but rather than partake in this incestuous relationship, she escapes to another kingdom. Eventually, she marries another king, thus avoiding marriage to her father.

In Woodman's interpretation of this fable, her mother's dying wish unwittingly entraps her husband in a ruinous relationship with his daughter. However, these circumstances are empowering to Allerleirauh, who develops the guile and cunning to free herself from her father and find a suitable lover.

Like Allerlierauh, I had been pressed into an unwanted relationship with my father. And like the queen, my mother had created the circumstances for this incestuous union to take root.

I have found this fable a useful way of understanding that I must free myself from the bonds of my abuse and take back the control I had lost or perhaps never really had.

I also began to realize that my father had made a kind of marital claim on me, as if I were his own special concubine and no one else's. In many ways, I felt like I was a second wife, fulfilling my father's sexual needs. Now, when I see my father at social functions, he does little more than stare at me. A kind of lingering mix of sadness and allurement now seems to fill him. Perhaps it is unresolved grief; perhaps it is a desire for his "property" to be returned to his lap.

As has been noted by others, his eyes follow me unabashedly around the room. This has only intensified in his declining years, as if his aging state has made it somehow permissible for him to try to reclaim me again, in those dark shark-like eyes of his.

In its fullest form, trust involves surrendering all we consider worthwhile and precious in ourselves. Trust should build confidence and a perpetual sense of certainty that revitalizes all our relationships.

I have never known such trust, not in my family, not in my life, not in myself. After much personal work, it came as a sobering thought to me that the abuse I had experienced would become a single point of reference that would shape all my ongoing relationships to men. It's of little wonder then that I came to believe love was just a game, rigged right from the start, just another one of those mirages in life that disappeared the closer you got to it.

Admittedly, some of the men I knew were quite lovely, while others were downright lousy. I started to find shared threads in respect to their own abusive relationships with their mothers, fathers, siblings, extended family, friends, and so on. In fact, so many of my relationships reflected these bonds of abuse that I could easily fill another book about them.

What I generally found in common with "my men" was their flawed thinking in terms of respect, gentility, and kindness. Some of these men would even talk about the factors that had ended their previous relationships, only to find them re-enacted in our own love story. It seemed that I was destined to continuously pick up the pieces as the supportive girlfriend.

In the end, I convinced myself I was somehow there just to deal with their issues while remaining ensnared in my own. And so I began to tick the same boxes time and time again: addict, alcoholic, adulterer, abuser. I began to attract the same old dysfunctional relationships, each seemingly with its own inevitable end date.

When it came to my husband, I really believed I had found true love. Like Allerleirauh, I wanted to finally escape my abusive bondage to my father, but unlike our astute princess, I did not take the time to form a healthy internal relationship. Instead, I went from one controlling, abusive man to another.

Ultimately, my mistake was that I had foisted all my idealized romantic notions onto my husband, transforming him into some kind of perfect spouse. Conveniently, I forgot—or maybe ignored—all those flaws that would become the death knell of our marriage.

Like my past experiences with men, I gave him too much of my personal power, too much of my money, and way too many of my own hopes and dreams. On and on it went until there was nothing left, just like it had always been, just as I'd always known.

And so I resolved to end this damaging way of relating to men by taking that first and perhaps most important step: self-forgiveness. Almost immediately, I began to rise, rise above myself, despite myself, to get off the merry-go-round of feeling small and broken, as I had felt with so many men.

No longer could I plead ignorance or play the victim. But I did need the time and space to begin a healing process in order to make amends to myself.

Time to tap.

Tapping Script 28

KC   Even though I have made some bad choices in relationships from desperate places, I love and forgive myself.

KC   Even though I have given up so much of my power to so many, I love and forgive myself.

KC   Even though I have placed myself time and time again in abusive relationships, I willingly open my heart to my own forgiveness.

EB   No longer will I say yes to them.

SE   That time is over.

UE   I did hand over my trust, and it was broken and betrayed.

UN   But I forgive myself for this.

CH   I did hand over my heart, and it was shattered.

CB   But I forgive myself for this.

UA   I did hand over my personal power.

TH   But I forgive myself for this.

EB   I did give up hope.

SE   But I forgive myself for this.

UE   I did hand over my money.

UN   But I forgive myself for this.

CH I did hand over my self-respect.

CB But I forgive myself for this.

UA I now take back my longing for their love.

TH For it was never worth longing for.

EB I take back my broken mind.

SE And mend the fences of my broken soul.

UE I take back my dreams.

UN Trampled underfoot.

CH I take back my own truth.

CB And will for now and ever speak it.

UA I will forget all their lies.

TH And forgive myself for believing them.

EB I forgive myself for giving.

SE When there was nothing given back.

UE I gave all that I had, but it was never enough.

UN So now I forgive myself.

CH I forgive myself.

CB I forgive myself.

UA [Your name], it's time to feel safe again.

TH All is forgiven, my love.

When we begin to heal what is broken within us, we truly start to see those in front of us. We move away from sowing the seeds of contempt, anger, and fear and start to make inroads into understanding others in their actuality, beyond our abuse.

So take heart!

There are ways and means to overcome these ingrained tendencies, such as using EFT to address and to reframe our own internal logic. Part of this requires us doing our best to correctly identify and name the true source of our pain and hurt, so that we remain on track to finding a genuine solution to any given problem in our relationship.

Though the issues may seem related to the original abuse or abandonment, they are not necessarily linked. What we attach to any sense of abuse may simply be acts of stupidity, selfishness, or inattention leading to a natural sense of disappointment.

We may even find we are viewing acts of kindness and compassion through the same filter, unable to determine if we are being cared for or being groomed for some ulterior motive. An important skill we need to learn then is to discern between what is actual and what is perceived abuse and abandonment in our relationship.

Exercise

The Hurt Meter

Draw four columns on a page.

In the first column, write down an action or event by your partner that has prompted a significant negative response in you.

For example, "He did not remember our anniversary."

In the second column, write down what link (if any) there is to your past sense of abuse or abandonment.

For example, "My (abusive) father never remembered my birthday."

If there is no link, write down the unrelated causes of your negative feelings in the third column. Consider what issues or causes may be linked to their own actions, independent of your past abuse.

For example, "My partner had a lot of work on that day and forgot about it."

In the fourth column, rank from 1 to 10 the intensity of your feelings about this event/action, 1 being negligible through to 10 being feelings of rage, terror, depression, and so on (e.g., 8 out 10).

Now again rank your feelings after considering whether they are linked to your past abuse and abandonment (e.g., 4 out of 10).

Prioritize the list, and focus upon the top three actions or events that have perceived links relating to past abuse issues.

Consider now,

- *How has your decision making impacted your past and present relationships?*
- *What steps may now differ in terms of how you relate to your partner?*
- *What level of blame or accountability does your partner now carry in relation to your past issues?*

Try to gauge just how linked the actions of your partner are to those of your past abuser(s). Is it clear and direct, or is there only a possible connection?

Let me point out that there is nothing wrong with relying upon our own intuition and wisdom based on past experiences. But one thing, as they say, doesn't necessarily have anything to do with the other. It can merely be that we are joining the dots in our mind in accordance with the root causes of our abuse and abandonment.

Let's do some tapping.

Tapping Script 29

KC   Even though my trust has been broken, time and time again, I love and accept myself.

KC   Even though the pain of abandonment is still with me, I love and accept myself.

KC   Even though I feel haunted by rejection, I accept myself and how I feel.

EB   All my grief of abandonment.

SE   All my grief of rejection.

UE   All my tears of heartache.

UN   They keep leaking from my body.

CH   And still, I feel.

CB   There are no safe arms around me.

UA   Even though (name partner) is here.

TH   I still feel the shame.

EB   I still feel the anger.

SE   I still feel the pain.

UE   All the tricks.

UN   All the lies.

CH   All the broken promises.

CB   My human heart needs trust.

UA   I make no apology for that.

TH   My inner child makes no apology for that.

EB   I need you here, [name partner].

SE   As a whole and caring man/woman.

UE   As the one who will stand by me.

UN   As the one who will rise.

CH   The one who will be my safe harbor.

CB   From all your misdeeds.

UA   And the misdeeds of my past.

TH   It is time to call it out.

EB   It's time to say what's what.

SE   I need you now.

UE	And not my past.
UN	I will let go of my demons.
CH	Who taunt our future.
CB	Who bring wrack and ruin to our relationship.
UA	But you must do your part too.
TH	You who are with me.
EB	You who claim to love me.
SE	Must help me rid myself.
UE	Of what does not belong here.
UN	It will speak no longer in our house.
CH	It will become a stranger to my soul.
CB	And to yours too, my love.
UA	To that I will promise.
TH	And try to keep the old ghosts from our door.
EB	What should have never been started.
SE	Can be ended.
UE	What should have never had a beginning.
UN	Will be no more.

CH   No more.

CB   No more.

UA   No more.

TH   The end is in sight.

Exercise

This next process will require some hard, honest thinking on your behalf. Let's start by listing your responses to the following essential elements of any relationship. Indicate anywhere along the double-arrow spectrum which negative or positive belief or value you tend to lean toward, in terms of your relationship. (Don't overthink it. Just respond quickly.) By signifying a response in the middle, you will be suggesting a neutral answer of "Not sure" or "Not Important."

Negative Belief/Value ⟵⟶ **Positive Belief/Value**

Disempowered ⟵⟶ **Empowered**

Inequality ⟵⟶ **Equality**

Loss of Freedom ⟵⟶ **Freedom**

Abusive ⟵⟶ **Respectful**

Loneliness ⟵⟶ **Companionship**

Lack of Intimacy ⟵⟶ **Intimacy**

Separate ⟵⟶ **Belonging**

Selfish ⟵⟶ **Sharing**

No Financial Control ⟵⟶ **Financial Control**

Now add in your own negative/positive responses tailored to your own relationship.

Looking over your responses,

- *Which aspects of your relationship are working well, and which require more work? How does this make you feel?*
- *How might these outcomes influence your future decision making and expectations regarding your relationship?*
- *How does this evaluation correspond to your own original notion of true love?*

If you feel comfortable, perhaps share your responses with a close friend or even with your partner. See whether his or her responses correspond with yours or perhaps provide fresh insights into the direction and priorities of your relationship.

Tapping time.

<u>Tapping Script 30</u>

KC   Even though my expectations have not always been met in my relationships, I love and accept who I am.

KC   Even though I feel like a failure sometimes in my relationships, I love and accept myself.

KC   Even though I sacrificed so many years to past relationships, I release myself from all these regrets.

EB   I gave up so much.

SE   I don't know how much more I can risk.

UE	So much was taken from me.
UN	I am scared of what is to come.
CH	I am scared of what [name partner] will do.
CB	Doesn't she or he understand what I have been through?
UA	I need a lot of convincing that she or he is safe.
TH	I need to know I can trust him or her.
EB	Perhaps it is time to trust myself more too?
SE	Perhaps it is time to look at myself more closely?
UE	Perhaps it is time to lower my walls?
UN	Perhaps it is time to stop keeping what I need inside?
CH	Perhaps it is time for my renewal.
CB	So that I will begin again.
UA	So that I can believe again.
TH	So that I can trust again.
EB	I am rewriting all the old rules.
SE	I am fixing all the old ways.
UE	The ones that took power away from me.
UN	In this, I will make a vow.

I See You

CH   To my goals.

CB   To my dream.

UA   To love.

TH   To honor.

EB   And to my own self-respect.

SE   Blessings on each of these vows.

UE   Blessings on myself.

UN   Blessings on my relationship.

CH   I know I can release all the broken parts of it to the light.

CB   Both past.

UA   And present.

TH   A new time is dawning.

EB   I will be the author of my own success.

SE   I will be the hero of my own story.

UE   I need no other to save me.

UN   I need no other to take control of my life.

CH   I am in control.

CB   What comes is all on me now.

UA   I am strong enough to say this now.

TH   Because I know my own way home.

Exercise

Another exercise recommended to me was to write a letter to my soul mate in a simple, conversational manner. In this way, I was able to unlock my own authentic notions of love.

Grab a pen and paper, and begin to shape your own letter to your soul mate. This may be someone you are yet to meet or a more fulfilling and complete version of your existing partner.

Write down a few key points in order to form the body of the letter. Once the letter is complete, read it aloud. Try to envisage your true soul mate materializing in your mind.

I chose to write mine during a beautiful full moon evening, full of bright, glowing stars, rugged up on my back porch in June 2017 at one thirty in the morning.

> *Dear Soul Mate / Husband,*
>
> *I write this letter to express to you how much I love you. I am so deeply grateful for our life together.*
>
> *You are the love of my life. Your humor, kindness, and emotional bravery continue to feed my heart and soul. I love how truly comfortable and safe I feel with you, with all my stories, past and present. You always accept me as I am. Our love is unconditional.*
>
> *You are my fire and my gold. But most of all, you are my best friend.*

I embrace our evening chats in bed, sharing our day while in the world. You are always interested in what I have to offer, big or small. Wherever we are, we always have fun. Though we may occasionally hit a bump in the road, our collective wisdom and compassion always see us through these challenges.

Thank you for being a great cook, a magnificent lover and hand holder, and just an overall great, sexy man! Our bedroom life is rich, passionate, and beautiful. I love being held by you and feeling that you are my safe place that I can surrender into.

You love my children, and they love you. I am grateful that we can share our financial prosperity. I love how you celebrate me and trust in me and I trust in you.

I hope we will live out our days together with an ever-deepening, cherishing love.

You are the golden link, the key to my heart.

Love always,

Brigit

I must confess at this point that the allure of my own inner Juliet still draws me to the magnetism and excitement of those first firecracker moments of romance. Being a divorcee, I accept that the institution of marriage failed me in the past. Yet this is still coupled with an acute sense of having missed out on my own happily ever after fairy tale.

Ultimately, I believe there is still a place for marriage or a soul mate in my life. I would be denying myself an opportunity of healing if I did not at least entertain the possibility of renewing a lifelong bond.

To do this, I have worked upon rekindling key aspects of this love and readied myself by examining the fundamentals of a healthy and positive relationship. In this way, I have begun to sweep away all those built-up negative thoughts and feelings that have accumulated over time and drawn closer to a better concept of a realistic lifelong partner.

Perhaps I may have listened to one too many gurus on this topic. However, what stood out for me as an essential teaching on this matter was the realization that I had to find my own language, my own words, in order to invite my soul mate into my life.

Whether or not you feel that this process will create a spiritual synergy with your lover is up to you. But understand, creating a sense of real love and authenticity is an essential component in aligning with any potential partners.

Ritual

Light a candle for the inner child.

Blessings on the inner child.

Blessing on the love yet to come.

Protect that which is most sacred.

Protect my heart within.

Keep it safe for those who most deserve it.

It is such a precious thing.

Blessed be.

Blessed be.

Blessed be.

CHAPTER 13
PATRIARCHAL SOIL

I KNOW MEN.

I have known them all my life, through the thick and the thin. I have lived with them as a sister, a daughter, a mother, a wife and a lover. They have beguiled and betrayed me, sometimes at the same time. I have given birth to them and watched them slowly wither away. I have witnessed their greatest triumphs and defeats. I have also witnessed their vilest acts.

I've washed, clothed, ironed for, fed, hugged, and dreamed with men. I have also been abandoned by them. They have been my greatest achievement and my greatest burden. At times, they have been my everything and then taken everything away from me. I have adored them and detested them in every conceivable way. They have, for better or worse, been integral to my life.

In short, I know my subject matter. And so I say to you now, this patriarchy, this God-given rights of men must go!

This very sober-sounding term has often been bandied about, particularly in the media and various sociopolitical arenas of debate. Perhaps it's time to own exactly what patriarchy means to us, as it is the foundation of our culture where men hold a greater portion of power over women.

In Western society, many of the precepts of the patriarchy can find their origins from this quote in the Bible: "Let your women keep silent in the churches, for they are not permitted to speak; but they are to be submissive, as the law also says" (1 Corinthians 14:34–35 Kings James Bible).

I believe it is a topic needing our clear and undivided attention. Moreover, much of the abuse I have discussed in previous chapters relates to this power imbalance enshrined in our society, turning women into second-class citizens.

Despite all the various social breakthroughs in recent times, it is still here among us, like a disease needing to be inoculated against and controlled. In my time as a therapist, I have worked with many women who feel trapped in what I call a "domestic depression." This condition is a kind of oppressive codependency, whereby they have surrendered to various forms of deprivation and abuse, in order to preserve their relationship to their male partners.

So perhaps the patriarchy is not out in the open as it once was, but it is enough to protect those men who uphold their right to control and discriminate socially, politically, and economically against women.

Guilt and shame have been a major tool in the patriarchy's arsenal used for centuries to keep the feminine oppressed and helpless. For women of my generation, it was *his* belief system that was whispered into us all our lives, as we slept, as we watched TV, as we watched ourselves, so much so that we became embedded with a toxic mix of the feminine, based upon half-truths and our supposed instinctual nurturing priorities. Subsequently, we have been laden with all manner of "womanly" responsibilities. We are judged, shamed, and chastened by

- how we should look
- what we should weigh
- how we should dress
- how we should act

And so it went.

The truth is, it is no good for anybody. Creating power imbalances never ends well, as history has consistently demonstrated. It is the basis upon which pain, humiliation, and discrimination are allowable.

Often kind and compassionate people are preconditioned to turn a blind eye to the excesses and abuses of the patriarchy. In the end, women and many men who do not meet its expectations are criticized and bullied. Sometimes, the patriarchy is enforced by other women, who seek safety, favor, or status within the hierarchy. My mother was one of them. All my life I have been buried in the patriarchal soil, trapped in its unforgiving wasteland.

Undeniably, my father was a hardworking breadwinner who undertook his accepted role in society dutifully, but his seemingly honorable intentions blanketed a deeper reality, a darker truth. He was prepared to not only block women in his family from having their own authentic voice, but he would sexually abuse them as if they were his chattels, his property to do with what he pleased.

By the time I reached adolescence, my natural desire to experiment with and explore different values and beliefs was quashed by my father. Any variation of his expectations of me was met with the sharp hackneyed threat of "My way or the highway!" Beyond this, the consequences of disobeying him ranged from being grounded through to being hit. All the while, my mother sat back on the sidelines or actively supported every one of his actions.

My father was not motivated by loving protection or nurturing guidance but by a need to indoctrinate me with the precepts of the patriarchy. Consciously or unconsciously, he was shaping me into something acceptable in a man's world, so much so that I would come to define myself as how my father saw me, as "the good little girl."

As touched upon in previous chapters, I was brought up to be the caregiver, the housewife, and the child maker. In my marriage, I adopted the role of "the good mother," while my ex-husband took on all the trappings and entitlements of the patriarchal father.

A significant aspect of his role was a sense of absolute authority over his children, including me. His weapon of choice to enforce his power was generally emotional abuse, abandonment, or neglect, served out in generous portions, especially when he was drunk. As was befitting of the times, I was largely left to bear the brunt of all of this alone. If I was to drill down into the core values of our marriage, the following would stand out for me the most:

His money is more important than my money.

His time to himself is more important than my time to myself.

His alcoholism is only a problem for me, and I must deal with the consequences of it.

He decides where to go on holiday, not me.

He decides where we live.

He spends the money as he decides, but I make sure all the bills are paid.

He owns my body. He has rights to it sexually.

I clean up after him.

I cook for him.

I look after his children. He plays with them when he wants to.

If I disagree with him, he can verbally abuse and intimidate me.

He is the leader. I am the follower.

If something goes wrong, it's never his fault.

If it's never his fault, I am just nagging him.

He will protect me but not from himself.

Exercise

Notably, these core values could easily be transferable between men and women, with similar imbalances in power. Are many of these core beliefs present in your relationship? How do they differ? List them.

Fortunately the patriarchy, this social malaise, so formidable in the past, is on its way out, imploding like a house of cards. However, this way of seeing the world must be actively challenged and the men upholding it chastised like any spoiled child because there is no longer any room, any plausible justification left for these kinds of men. They can no longer plead ignorance or make claim to any special kind of entitlement.

We are at the cusp of a new age, one in which a whole new belief system needs to promote what is best for both genders and for all forms of sexual identity. And so now, I say to any man still clinging to the patriarchy, "Time's up, gentlemen."

Just as in chapter 5, "I Am Worth My Next Breath," I want you to focus again on saying no in the following tapping script and exercise. However, this time, you are specifically focusing upon those men and women who have exercised or condoned patriarchal control in your life.

Let's do some tapping.

Tapping Script 31

KC   Even though [name of person] has made it unsafe for me to say, "No!" I love and accept myself.

KC   Even though [name of person] has told me to accept his or her choices over mine, I love and accept who I am.

KC Even though I was raised to believe that [name of person] is in charge of me, I will now free myself from this narrow way of thinking.

EB Yet, who am I to say no?

SE No to [name the person]?

UE No to anyone?

UN I have been taught to obey.

CH I have been taught to refer to [name the person] before making a decision.

CB Can I trust myself to know what's best for me?

UA I'm not familiar with full independence.

TH I am scared to separate from [name the person].

EB I fear being alone.

SE I fear [name the person] will no longer love me if I say no.

UE I'm not smart enough to stand up on my own.

UN Or lead the way to create my own destiny.

CH I have always been told what to think.

CB I have always been told what to feel.

UA I have been taught that the world is a dangerous place.

TH Without [name the person] by my side.

EB	I do want something different now.
SE	I want to be independent.
UE	I can just start imaging saying yes to my needs and wants.
UN	I can start to feel the relief in making my own choices.
CH	Just saying yes out loud to what I want feels empowering.
CB	I know of others who have said no to their parent or partner.
UA	Why can't I?
TH	I will plant this word deep inside of myself.

EB	So that one day no one will stop my nos.
SE	That little word.
UE	It is so powerful.
UN	That little word.
CH	Gives me hope.
CB	That little word.
UA	Gives me dignity.
TH	Just thinking about it gives me joy!

EB	In a way I have never known before.
SE	Society says it's okay for me to say it.

UE   The law says it's okay for me to say it.

UN   I am saying it's okay for me to say it.

CH   So I will!

CB   Because I am free now to stand in my own power.

UA   We all have the right to say no.

TH   Only then can we all say *yes*!

Exercise

How good are you at saying, "No to …!"

Here are some places you may care to start:

No to [name abuser]

No to [name enablers] (i.e., those who directly or indirectly allowed you to be abused)

No to being financially blackmailed

No to you not being there for me

No to the silence

No to your undermining ways

No to your sense of entitlement

No to your bigoted views

No to the pubic hair left in the basin

No to you always interrupting me

No to your slamming doors

No to your empty beer cans in my garden

No to being ignored

No to not making the bed

No to being rude to my friends

No to your condescending tone

No to the toilet seat always being left up

No to your stupid grin

No to that sullen stare

No to the bruises on my arms

No to your rolling eyes

No to your dishes left in the sink

No to your sarcastic slurs

No to being pushed up against the wall

No to making any more excuses for you

No to the lies you tell me

No to lies you tell yourself

No to you knowing everything

No to you telling me I'm "a bitch"

No to having sex with you

No to you never turning up on time

No to not being heard

No to you not seeing me

And finally, no to all your no's!

Write your own list of "No to…"

Now stand in a room with a trusted friend or counselor and take turns saying, "No to …" while the other person is silent and listens. Some laughing and awkward moments are likely in this exercise. But that's fine. Have some fun. Just remember, this is your way of overcoming your own preconditioning that has kept you compliant, passive, and silent.

Start off softly and build up your, "No to …" to a powerful, convincing, "No to …!" Give yourself permission to say each statement loudly and with conviction.

Okay, when you are ready, let loose from every fiber, from every cell in your body.

Time to say, "No! No! No!"

Notice how you are standing. Do you feel different? Perhaps your feet are now planted more solidly on the ground? As you say it, monitor your breathing and your heart rate. Notice where your hands are each time you say it. Are they on your hips or perhaps curled up tight into a fist? Take note of the tension in your body. Has it decreased? Maybe you have created more stress? Keep repeating this exercise for a couple of days, maintaining a mental body scan of yourself.

At the heart of much abuse is the denial of the opportunity to experience the world with a true sense of one's own identity and authenticity. To sugarcoat this imbalance, the patriarchy often seeks to portray itself as the provider, the wise, and the protector, the one who really knows what's going on and what's best for you.

Many women have been trained to accept their place in society as some kind of controlling dictum of nature, as simply the way it is or the way it has always been. Yet for many of us, we have known innately that this way of understanding the world is flawed. In fact, it has indirectly been an enabler of abuse.

We need to understand that our true feminine nature has been hemmed in by restrictive, often suppressive processes and practices. This has prohibited women from exploring their own unique qualities, including our preferences, our fantasies, and our own desires, beyond what is considered proper and acceptable to our gender.

However, we all know of men who cannot, will not, loosen their bonds to the patriarchy. They simply either have too much to lose or too little to gain. They will do their utmost to hold on to their historical "right to rule," which is simply not open to discussion.

They come from all ages and socioeconomic backgrounds. Their behaviors can range from passive and controlling through to outright abusive. They sometimes want revenge for a deep hurt or to make up for their own sense of powerlessness by striking out at those closest to them. Most refuse to seek professional help, instead opting to remain insulated in their own misogynistic views.

Brick by brick, lie by lie, we must dismantle the patriarchy, these values, these beliefs that have been the foundation for so much abuse. It is time we all undertook an intensive examination of who we are as human beings, in order to usurp this tired old paradigm that has defined us for so long.

No longer will we stay silent and small, accepting only the crumbs off the patriarchy's plate. No longer will we accept that *he* alone is to be revered, that *he* alone will be loved above all things, that it is *his* needs to be placed before all others.

Whether implicitly or overtly, some women have been taught to be competitive with each other. Jealousy is often at the root of this rigged game, and it generally runs deep, introduced into our unconsciousness long ago. Jealousy feeds into every feeling of insecurity and lack. Mother to daughter, woman to woman, we attack each other from places of envy, helplessness, anger, and abandonment. Instead of protecting each other, we can end up fighting amongst ourselves like gladiators in a Roman Coliseum, creating a useful distraction from our true enemy.

But things are changing. Social justice advocacy groups, such as the #MeToo movement, have given us the courage that we can challenge and debase the abusive powers of the patriarchy, stripping it of its once invincible sources of control. It is their example, as well as those of other individuals and groups, that we should turn to for inspiration and courage.

And so, the hope must be that this rising tide of universal freedom will eventually wash away the patriarchy, turning it into just another social relic of the past, like the chastity belt and the corset.

Exercise

To stand up for, support, and encourage one another is a clear pathway to healing. But we must see ourselves first for what we are and what we will be.

For a moment, just look at yourself in the mirror. Whatever your sex or orientation, just come to realize we are all cogs within the same patriarchal machine.

Put aside all that, and just see yourself for what you are.

Let yourself shine. Let that "you" in the mirror know it's okay to love yourself and celebrate this love by giving it to yourself first and then giving it to others who deserve you.

Now draw in close to your own reflection and whisper firmly back to yourself, "He is not in control of me. I am in control of me. We are all equal."

Each time you say these words, breathe deeply ... in and out, in and out, in and out.

Keep breathing, and whisper these words. Let them settle deep inside.

Okay, let's do some tapping now.

<u>Tapping Script 32</u>

KC   Even though it hasn't been safe for me to be my true self, I love and accept myself.

KC   Even though others have not given me the safe harbor I need, I love and accept myself.

KC   Even though I have been locked into *his* choices, *his* wants, *his* needs, I forgive myself.

EB   I am exhausted by all the energy it takes to serve.

SE   I feel overwhelmed by life.

UE   I want to be free to be me.

UN   I want to express myself without being punished by the patriarch.

CH	I *will* fight.
CB	This is worth fighting for!
UA	I am inspired to seek my true self.
TH	I am inspired to seek my real goals.

EB	I release the fear from the cells of my body.
SE	I release the unconscious fog from my mind.
UE	I choose to stay awake now.
UN	I have a right to feel protected and loved in my relationships.
CH	With both men and women.
CB	I have a right to stand on equal ground with any man.
UA	I can be as big, bold, and seen in the world as I want.
TH	I will be cheered on by all women and men as I succeed.

EB	Of all creeds, of all colors, of all ages.
SE	Yes.
UE	Yes.
UN	Yes.
CH	I say yes to being *big* in this world!
CB	I say yes to being *bold* in this world!

UA   And I say yes to being seen in this world!

TH   I promise myself, now and forever, to stand fully with the feminine.

In ancient European traditions, the old women, or crones, were considered as seers of knowledge and wisdom, openly revered in their communities. However, like the word *hag* (derived from the word *hagio* meaning "holy") or *witch* (derived from the word *wit* meaning "wise"), this word too was hijacked, so it became a demeaning term for an ugly old woman.

Sadly, the patriarchy has stifled the potential for us to learn from so many cultures, which would have given us a unique perspective of the female experience throughout the ages. Sadly, much of this knowledge has been left to waste away, unseen and forgotten.

Far too many of our sisters have gone to the grave based upon the flimsy precepts of patriarchy. Desperate, alone, and silent, they have been locked into this terrible conspiracy of men that opposes their minds, bodies, and souls. Some aspects would be laughable today if they hadn't had such deep, far-reaching consequences.

My ultimate rescue from the patriarchal web happened five years ago when I finally read a book that I had owned for twenty-five years. It was *Women Who Run with the Wolves*, by Clarissa Pinkola Estes. She is a Jungian analyst and a *cantadora*, which in Spanish means "a keeper of old stories."

As I first attempted to read the book, I distracted myself with numerous cups of tea, small walks, and several quick phone calls. Finally, I realized I had actively avoided turning over the first page for almost two hours. An inner patriarchal voice screamed, "What is this? Stop reading! You are breaking the rules! Stop this, Brigit!"

I knew then that some part of me was withholding from Estes's wisdom. When I recognized what was happening, I decided to read the chapter out loud as a way of standing my ground. As I read her words, I was in awe of how she nourishes and understands women and, moreover, how she has their back. Upon reflection, I was able to begin disconnecting from the patriarchal maze in my mind and accessing the archetypical power of the wild woman within.

By the end of the first chapter, my foggy dissociation and years of preconditioning were lifting. The inner voice could no longer keep out the truth, and so this book became like a Bible to me. It was all I read, and slowly but surely, I started to wake up. Dreams would arise from my subconscious as I slept, whereby I was becoming the rescuer and not the victim.

My waking life increasingly became one in which I could set healthy boundaries toward my male friends, family, and even an ex-lover with whom I was struggling to assert myself. This also encompassed old enemies from my past, the giants and demons in my psyche whom I would no longer let defeat me. At times, her words felt strangely familiar but somehow forgotten, as if she was leading me to parts unknown in myself, lost down some Jungian well of collective feminine consciousness.

For me, Estes provides stories that express the true order of things, encompassing respect, loyalty, and love in all its equal parts central to any intimate relationship between the masculine and the feminine.

Many of the missing pieces and buried strengths that I sought lay in Estes's book. As I read it, I felt like I was snuggled up and safe on the lap of the great archetypical mother, engrossed in the intrigue and beauty of each word and phrase.

In one of the chapters, she wrote of a tale called "The Skeleton Woman," based upon an Inuit myth how a father discards his daughter in the sea when he is disappointed in her. His daughter's flesh rots away, and she becomes only bones, lying on the ocean floor. One day, a young fisherman, new to the area and unaware of the tales of the haunted bay, catches her bones in his fishing line. He feels the weight of a catch and eagerly winds in his line, only to be confronted by her emerging grotesque and terrifying form. He then runs home in shock and fear, not looking back.

However, unknown to the terrified fisherman she remains entangled in his precious line, and is dragged all the way into the safety of his home. In the light of the fire that he lit, he sees her tangled mess before him, and in time he begins to feel his fear soften. Finally, he pulls her bones out of his fishing line one by one and carefully places them back together in the right order. All the while, he hums a calming tune.

Skeleton Woman is soothed by his kindness and attention. When he finally falls asleep, she drinks a tear from his eye and is nourished back into life. She then borrows his heart and places it inside her rib cage, this allows her flesh to grow back and take the shape of her feminine form once more.

When the fisherman awakes, he finds himself lying next to her. She is full, womanly, and magnificent. They make love and form an enduring relationship. From that time on, the Skeleton Woman having been once a part of the sea, is able to guide the fisherman to the best fishing spots, allowing them both to prosper with food and income.

This story demonstrates when a man learns to truly open his heart and bravely tend to the patriarchal wounds of the woman a deeply nourishing and sustaining union is created.

In many ways, the patriarchal conditioning stands in the way of men realizing this kind of potential in relationships. The fisherman surrenders his heart to the wounded daughter thrown out to sea by her father. He saw his daughter as his to discard. My father saw me as his to touch and have claim over. Yet a healing is possible.

Though this next exercise is largely directed to my female readers, I'd ask that we all come to understand that the patriarchy is a shared toxic inheritance of abandonment and abuse that has dishonored us all. Therefore, I respectfully ask that our male readers join in bringing about the equality and diversity of life we all richly deserve. If you truly stand in the masculine, then you will give to us your whole heart—no matter what your fear, no matter what the cost, just like Estes's fisherman. Only then will we all prosper.

Exercise

Close your eyes and take a moment to envisage a positive masculine figure in your life. You could choose your actual father or a father from a movie or a book. Choose a memory where you have been abused or abandoned by the masculine, and allow this positive masculine figure to move toward you with his beating heart. Imagine him placing it inside your chest.

Try to imagine the heart beating inside you now. Hear it beating as your grief, abandonment, or sorrow begins to subside and the "new flesh" grows around it. Feel the unconditional love of the masculine working its way through your body.

Breathe and surrender to it.

Men have used their religions and institutions to pacify and sanction women for a millennium. This process has been reinforced through the arts, the media, and various mythologies. In all of these things, women have been seen, heard, and considered through his filter of control. No matter what seemingly positive notions of women, men have dreamed up, they are still a means to reinforce his dominance. Subsequently, there are but a few examples in history in which men have fully embraced the true feminine essence.

For this reason, we need to generate more stories like the ones in Estes's book, ones that usurp the traditional tales of the patriarchy, imbuing them with feminine strength, courage, beauty, and wisdom.

We, the wild women of this world, must begin to win back that which was actively destroyed and ultimately lost. I am thankful this is becoming more a reality in this day and age, as we don't have to burn our bras, and they certainly can't burn us at the stake anymore.

We also ask that men come to regard our bodies like a temple rather than a brothel, to understand that the patriarchal version of the feminine is largely a myth built upon manipulation, objectification, and distortion of women. We, beautiful, sweet sisters, should be respected and embraced exactly as we are, at every cycle of our existence, wrinkles and all, guys!

Let go of the fear and shame that has been propagated within you simply because you were born a female. By drawing out the old poison within the patriarchal soil, we can begin to cultivate the new pure seeds, born of the feminine.

The time has come for us to rouse ourselves from the harmful delusions and slurs of our own inner critic, especially when it is acting as the wretched mouthpiece of the patriarchy. So be patient, be vigilant, and, most of all, stand tall.

Ritual

Light the candle for your inner child.

Read a page from Estes's book.

Let them hear the fables born of the feminine.

Drink in her wisdom

Dream of the freedom.

So that all shall live,

life to the fullest.

CHAPTER 14
THE "F" WORD

IN THIS FINAL chapter, I am hoping to help you create the opportunity to cut through what you may have been grappling with for months, years, or even decades. In short, I want you to find your own solutions back to yourself, your own way home.

Throughout this book, I have tried to awaken what was once silent as the result of abuse. It is a bond we share, mapped out in a common lineage that only those who have been in our situation can truly understand. We are now at a crossroad, you and I, one where we are embarking on a new beginning, leaving the past behind.

Understand, it is never too late to begin this process, never too late to be heard. It is time for the final phase, the final strategy: a pathway into forgiveness.

Exercise

The Greek translation of forgiveness literally means "to let go." Further explanations include, "to stop feeling anger toward someone, to stop blaming someone, and to stop feeling anger about some event or occurrence."

Take a moment now to notice what you feel in your body as you read this definition. What kinds of thoughts begin to arise, both negative and positive?

Write it all down before continuing this chapter.

In many ways, learning about forgiveness is like learning a new language. Initially it may seem completely foreign to us. However, when we start to forgive, we begin to grasp the full possibility of really taking back control of what we have become and who we are becoming.

However, moving into states of forgiveness can be a very arduous process, one that must be completed in a clear, wise and methodical manner. In preparation, we must first learn to tap into what is highest and most developed in us, both psychologically and philosophically.

To this end, it is an undertaking reserved for the adult part rather than the inner child, which carries the unfiltered vulnerability of past abuses. We must think, do, and act in a way that may seem counter-intuitive to our inner child, perhaps even threatening. Unlike the other chapters, we must begin this journey alone, protecting that which is most precious within us from first great storms of change.

Admittedly, my natural inclination is to say "F★★k you!" rather than "Forgive you," in respect to my abusers. But ask yourself this simple question: "How many times can one say that?" For so long, this was my main survival strategy for dealing with the accumulated hate and resentment I felt building up, year after year.

At first, it felt like a direct way to connect with those feelings that I was not able to access. At other times, it protected me, creating healthy boundaries and expectations with those who sought to abuse or sexually exploit me. And so the notion of being open to forgiveness only seemed to rob me of the little power I had. Yet now I know it was a fake power, a temporary fix for what had happened to me in the past.

Other questions arose in my mind:

- How much time and effort have I put into maintaining my sense of hate and anger?
- What has it cost me in terms of my relationships and connectedness to others?
- How much has it skewed my perception of the actions and statements of others? Have they always been fair and accurate?

- Has it affected my ability to genuinely feel love and feel kindness to its fullest extent?

What I've come to understand so far is that I have seen much of my life through a jaded lens of anger, a love-hate relationship, which is really, really difficult to be parted from.

Yet it has cost me a great deal of personal time and energy to maintain my anger and my hurt. I know its capacity to serve and protect me has now passed. In the end, what I originally wore like a badge of honor for the abuse is now just a dead weight around my shoulders.

And so this way of being was like a knight standing guard, manning the walls and barricades of my own self-preservation. This had left me in a kind of hypervigilant limbo, forever waiting for the next attack.

The drawbridge was definitely up.

I can only now see this for what it truly was. This was no castle but a prison of fear, informing my every thought, my every action, on a daily basis.

Of course, my inner critic was having a field day, basking in all this glorious bitterness. Any attempts to weaken or question it have been met with jeers of "See, you are being weak! You are standing by the appeasers. You are standing by the abusers! I've got your back here! Abuse deserves abuse. They all deserve it! Stand up for yourself, Brigit!"

I now understand that it was blocking me from the healing and peace I desperately craved. And so it was, to my great dismay, I was discovering that the first person I needed to forgive was in fact myself.

Forgiveness releases us from the bondages of resentment, so much so that we can discover a new prosperity of the heart. It is only then that we can unburden ourselves from the past in order to free ourselves for the future.

Okay, that's a lot to take in if you have never considered this line of thinking before. So let us begin to tap by just acknowledging the immediate challenge of even considering forgiveness.

Keep tapping, using this script until the idea of self-forgiveness finds a starting point within you. Do it as gently as possible; there is much tenderness and faith needed here. Let your love find a way.

Tapping Script 33

KC Even though just thinking about forgiveness brings on waves of anger in my body, I love and accept who I am.

KC Even though I am afraid that forgiving myself will let my offenders off the hook, I will try to embrace this possibility.

KC Even though this way of thinking seems so wrong for me, I now know that I need to consider it.

EB All this tightness in my body.

SE I don't want this conversation of forgiveness.

UE I don't see why I have to forgive anyone.

UN Being abused is not my fault!

CH So why should I forgive anyone?

CB What happened to me was inexcusable.

UA I want justice.

TH I want revenge.

I See You

EB   Isn't that the voice of a powerful person?

SE   How can I do this?

UE   How can I begin to wrap my brain around this one?

UN   Why does letting go of the hate and anger seem so hard?

CH   My refusal to forgive has been my way of surviving.

CB   My refusal to forgive has been my refuge.

UA   I haven't known how to feel safe without it.

TH   It's like a boulder in my [name body part].

EB   It lives.

SE   In me.

UE   Many names are engraved upon it.

UN   Those who abused me.

CH   And those who did not protect me.

CB   It's so heavy!

UA   You have no idea!

TH   No light can get through.

EB   How can I even trust forgiveness will work?

SE   God, this boulder!

UE Doesn't it keep me safe?

UN As I stand next to this boulder, it casts a shadow over me.

CH It feels like I have known nothing else.

CB Such a big boulder.

UA Such a big shadow.

TH I think it's time to see past it.

EB Can I see past it?

SE It feels so hard.

UE This boulder, this heaviness.

UN I can't go on like this.

CH This boulder.

CB This jagged rock of hate.

UA I think it's time.

TH Time to try forgiveness.

EB Oh God, I deserve this!

SE To dream of seeing things differently.

UE To dream of a healed soul.

UN	To feel emotionally whole.
CH	And you know what? I can do this!
CB	I can break the boulder.
UA	I can break the chains.
TH	I will be free from my pain.
EB	With each tap.
SE	I will free myself from anger.
UE	With each tap.
UN	I will free myself from resentment.
CH	With each tap.
CB	I am growing stronger now.
UA	I hear the boulder crack open, as I open.
TH	I begin to feel the potential of forgiveness.
EB	This is the time.
SE	I will free myself from pain.
UE	This is the time.
UN	I will begin to live in grace.
CH	This is the time.

CB   I will begin to live without hate.

UA   This is the time.

TH   The time of my forgiveness.

Well done, dear reader.

Just remember, what you are trying to achieve is so huge, wherever you have got up to in this process is okay. It is simply an opportunity for you to stop feeling wounded.

Keep tapping using this script as many times as you want. Adapt it to meet your own needs, your own specific wants. Take the time to consider that even the smallest seeds of grace and tolerance will begin to "break the boulder" within. Remember, you are unburdening a great deal of anger, pain, and resentment. So please be kind to yourself.

"Letting go and letting God in" is a phrase I have heard many times before. Whether we hold mystical beliefs or not, making a space in our soul creates not only new possibilities of healing, but allows us to acknowledge those aspects we should be grateful for.

Gratitude is a crucial component to our healing, since it allows us to see our own life from new perspectives, helping us emerge from the confines of our past abuse. However, to feel gratitude requires a genuine act of inner bravery, a revolution from within.

Most of us live our lives in shades of gray, whereby there is a constant flux and flow of both good and bad, light and darkness. Therefore, part of making inroads into forgiveness, is to acknowledge we need not be dominated by our past misery and that there is, in fact, much out there for us to be thankful for.

In essence, gratitude nurtures our ability to forgive and let go and ignite our excitement and positivity, making us appreciative of the small things that show up for us everyday. For me, my way of finding gratitude is to keep a journal reminding me of the simple wonders that exist all around us.

This can consist of being thankful for the air I breathe, the flowers in my garden, splinters of warm light at dawn, the food in my belly, the roof over my head, the hug of a loved one, the birthday surprise, and the smile of a stranger.

On other days, I will write about the amazing sessions I have spent making breakthroughs with my clients and the great privilege I have to witness their stories. I also write of the love and generosity shown to me by my friends and family.

Exercise

What simple, funny things can you think of that bring moments of joy and happiness in your life? Keep writing them down in a journal or place them on your altar to remind you.

We must start to think and then act upon each and every opportunity to find sources of gratitude in our lives. Ultimately, our goal is to become an emotional athlete, with our everyday acting as the gym. Thus, we will excel with each new challenge that is presented to us, filling us up with nourishing sources of delight and joy

However, our primitive brain is wired not to work this way. It wants to insulate us from the unpleasantness of this world, maintaining a "fortress mentality" against it. Therefore, it may interpret the action of gratitude as a means of weakening this position, thereby setting us up to be vulnerable to further abuse.

EFT is a useful tool to short-circuit this instinctual response, thereby creating the basis for a peaceful transition into higher states of being, giving us a different way of relating to our past. So much so, that we are able to finally reassure our primitive brain, "The world is not as bad as you think, and there is much within it to be thankful for."

In the end, our intention, is to find a way back to our pure, authentic self, the way we were meant to be before the trauma. This means ending all the anger, all the fear, all the critical conversations that have spread through our minds and bodies like a cancer, poisoning the way we see ourselves and the world around us.

I have worked both sides of the fence in terms of dealing with abusers and the abused. The truth is the abuser does not really get away with anything, even if never publicly exposed or prosecuted. In my experience, abusers generally carry within themselves levels of woundedness and dysfunction that have marked their lives.

Their sense of entitlement only serves to indicate that they are sick, in their minds, in their hearts, and in their souls. Even if there is no sense of outward remorse, they have often encased themselves in the same hell that first compelled them into partaking in their vile acts.

It then begs the question, why should you, you who did no wrong, continue to be smeared by the abusers' transgressions? If you think upon this, forgiveness becomes a conscious act of good old-fashioned defiance, since you are choosing to draw a line under those parts of your life.

You are providing yourself with the means to take back the control he or she has taken from you, giving you a real opportunity to transform your future. We can then begin to flourish, to break new ground and generate new hope for ourselves.

Before I continue, can I reiterate that forgiveness is not a "get-out-of-jail" card for your abuser or those who did not stand by you. It is simply a means of drawing a line in the sand, effectively giving you the means to put aside all those past things that no longer have a place in your life today.

Let us begin this pathway into forgiveness.

If possible, the first step is to analyze the origins of your abuser, and those who abandoned you. This will mean impartially looking at the facts at hand in a reasoned and objective manner. We must then consider the given circumstances of his or her upbringing, as well as the culture, values and belief systems that shaped them.

I acknowledge that we may have little or no understanding of our abuser's origins. In such cases, this can be a much tougher road to travel. However, whatever fragments of knowledge you can procure, all of it will stand you in good stead as you seek a pathway to forgiveness. For me, starting this very personal process meant understanding how my parents were shaped by their family history and background.

Let me begin by saying there is no map or qualification for being a good parent. Most of us are largely left to wing it, in our given time, place, and historical context. This applies to my parents, my grandparents, my great-grandparents, and so on down the line. Some of us may have improved on the quality of the parenting we experienced; others just repeat the same mistakes. Just understand that you, right now, can begin to break the cycles of abuse and abandonment that may have been going on for centuries. Quite a thought really.

So let me take you into my story, starting with my mother's side of the family. My grandmother was eighteen years old, facing the shame and public humiliation of being pregnant out of wedlock in 1930. She lived in a place and time that was dominated by a strict Catholicism and patriarchal social norms. "Gran," as we called her, was looked upon as a whore, and my mother was referred to as a "bastard child." Gran's father had passed away when she was thirteen, leaving her mother to raise six children on her own.

Despite being a single parent, struggling to raise a newborn baby, she remained a young woman at heart, wanting some fun and excitement in life. Her need to maintain her social identity and independence apparently led to negative consequences for my mother.

Stories of my mother's abandonment were passed between generations. One of them that I heard was when my great-aunty climbed through a window at night after hearing the anguished cries of my mother, who had been left home alone.

She eventually married and then divorced without having any more children. At some point, my great-grandmother intervened and reared my mother on her own. Subsequently, my mother's only sense of connection to her mother was steeped in sadness and abandonment.

Over time, my gran isolated herself further from her family, leaving my mother to be raised like an orphan, with neither her mother nor father contributing to her physical or emotional well-being. She also had no brothers or sisters to play with and therefore only had experiences of extended family bonds.

I remember my mother's deep shame and resentment, as Gran would rarely send a birthday card or visit. When I finally met her as a child, I recalled how she was a large woman coated in thick makeup and furs, smelling of mothballs. As a young adult, I would go visit her, often finding Gran steeped in urine, having drunk herself into an alcoholic stupor.

And so all this entrenched ancestral hurt, all this shame and abandonment, had existed long before I even came into being. For my mother, it was largely because she did not receive the love and support of her two natural parents. For my gran, it came from having lost her father early on and the isolation and shame from her family.

As for my great-grandmother, I can only presume she would have felt some level of disappointment and resentment, having been locked into rearing a child who was not truly hers.

As previously mentioned, research indicates that pain and trauma may influence the DNA structure within families. I believe as much as I have my mother's brown eyes, I have also inherited her acute sense of abandonment.

My mother was taught by nuns at a strict Catholic school. They would smack her left hand in order to make her write right-handed. This punishment left her so terrified she never felt able to learn to read or write properly.

As such, she never had the education or life experiences that would have helped her succeed in any of her own personal dreams or goals, beyond raising a family. Money was also scarce without a man's income, so all her factory wages would go toward the household. She worked until she was married at the age of twenty-two.

Even though my mother could not drive a car and relied completely on my father for finances, she managed to raise eight children. All of this occurred with little or no parental support or modelling. However, there was never any sense of celebration of this incredible achievement, certainly nothing that was ever conveyed to me as a child or adult. Parenting was simply a requirement, an acceptable way of being that she needed to get through.

It is perhaps timely to remember that our mothers' inner wounds are often a reflection of our own. I now see, and feel, that my mother did the best she could, coping with all her mother's abandonment and unmet needs.

What chance then did she have to acquire the skills needed to optimize her mothering? As I began to perceive my mother this way, it became easier to embrace the necessary steps toward healing and forgiving her.

My father's childhood was also a difficult one. He was born in 1925 in Northern Ireland in the midst of deeply entrenched sectarian unrest. He would recall soldiers patrolling the street and the brutal discrimination meted out toward him and his friends simply for being Catholic. People on both sides of this conflict were being maimed, killed, and tortured. It had been going on for centuries as an accepted way of life.

His father was a man of humble means who carted hay for a living. He was chronically unwell, suffering from severe untreated asthma as a result of the horsehair and hay. My father would tell us how he would regularly collect his dad drunk from the pub in order to get him home for dinner. My grandfather eventually died at the young age of forty-two.

Two years beforehand, he was terminally sick. This forced my father to leave school at fourteen to help provide an income for the family. My dad always wanted to continue on with education since he loved learning. And despite his teachers' protestations, his mother compelled him into becoming a milkman full-time.

This work required him to start at four each morning, even during the freezing Irish winters. Throughout this time, my grandfather continued to drink away my father's hard-earned wages. And so it was, a family of seven children and their mother were left to fend for themselves when he died.

Unfortunately, my grandfather's alcoholism was an all too common feature of Irish culture at the time, one that my father was unable to resist. He never felt close to his dad, and I cannot recall even one kind story about him. What I do know was that my grandfather physically abused my father as a form of punishment, just as my father did with me and my siblings.

When I met one of his brothers in my thirties, I was immediately struck by the same feeling of sexual depravity my father conveyed toward me when he was drunk. It was as if they both carried the same bad seed, the same corruption that led to their sense of sexual entitlement and lack of personal boundaries.

My guess is that schooling provided some measure of emotional and physical safety for my father, which he lost when he was forced out to work. I would also surmise that his own father's hidden emotional wounds and premature death did not equip my father adequately to deal with the sudden influx of adult responsibilities thrust upon him. It is also important to consider that my father would have been exposed to an array of potentially challenging and abusive situations as a teenager while working in an adult world.

Broken hearts and dreams and other forms of intergenerational wounding have long been a common feature of my family's masculine line. Even in his nineties, there remains a quiet suffering in my father, one that is hard to define.

I am also yet to work out exactly why I, and another sister, were picked out to be the "special" ones, the ones he thought it would be okay to sexually abuse. At this stage, I am unlikely to fully resolve the many enigmas that have dominated my life and my father's. Suffice to say, it has left me with far more questions than answers. This, it would seem, would be our lot together, his final legacy to me.

Exercise

Write down the story of each your significant ancestral family members who may have played a part directly in your life.

Consider the following:

- *What were the details that shaped their lives?*
- *What abuse or abandonment issues do you think they encountered?*
- *How old were they when given significant events/issues were taking place?*
- *Who else was involved?*
- *Does this impact upon your own view of them?*
- *How do you feel in your body as you complete this task (e.g., dismayed, relieved, dissociated, and so on)?*
- *What are the personal traits that you have in common with your parents and ancestors?*
- *How has their story played out in your life?*
- *What conclusions can you draw?*
- *Does it alter how you feel about your own abuse or abandonment?*

Now try to look back through your family tree as far as you can. Remember, many family stories may be steeped in lies, secrets, exaggerations, and myth. However, even these things contain within them a grain of truth that shapes a family's values and beliefs.

It may also be worthwhile accessing family records and other broader historical data through websites such as Ancestry.com. This will help you develop a better context of the economic, cultural, and historical events that impacted upon your family (e.g., war, stock market crash, disease, natural disasters, political upheaval, and so on).

Let's try some tapping.

Tapping Script 34

Think of someone you have identified in the previous exercise who you feel should have protected you or who has abused you. Now say that person's first name followed by each of the tapping points. Adapt the tapping points to fit your own specific situation.

EB	[name the person]	I see and feel your struggles.
SE	[name the person]	I see and feel your abandonment.
UE	[name the person]	I see and feel your deep shame.
UN	[name the person]	I see and feel your anger.
CH	[name the person]	I see and feel your emotional pain.
CB	[name the person]	I see and feel your neediness.
UA	[name the person]	I see and feel your rejection.
TH	[name the person]	I see and feel your low self-esteem.

I See You

EB	[name the person]	I see and feel your envy.
SE	[name the person]	I see and feel your fear.
UE	[name the person]	I see and feel your abuse.
UN	[name the person]	I see and feel your failings.
CH	[name the person]	I see and feel your confusion.
CB	[name the person]	I see and feel your poor boundaries.
UA	[name the person]	I see and feel your unspoken stories.
TH	[name the person]	I see your abuse.
EB	[name the person]	You are not alone.
SE	[name the person]	You are being seen by me.
UE	[name the person]	I am with you now.
UN	[name the person]	You are being heard.
CH	[name the person]	I know you have suffered too.
CB	[name the person]	Your childhood suffering was not your fault.
UA	[name the person]	Your story counts.
TH	[name the person]	I see your inner child now.

How does that make you feel? If you still experience a strong resistance to its intention, change or soften the tapping script or direct it to another family member. Understand that you alone are controlling this process of renewal and forgiveness. So take all the time you need to make it work, and, please, go gently on yourself.

Try stepping back now and reframing what happened to you and how it happened. For example, rather than thinking your mother didn't care about you, consider changing this thinking to she did not know *how* to care for you. Part of this process could then include *why* this was the case.

Return now to the idea that you are overturning repeated situations of abandonment and abuse that have perhaps echoed down through the generations in one form or another. Try to perceive that your ancestors may not have been entirely in control or lacked an understanding that the choices they were making were actually wrong. This part of the equation cannot be changed, but you can at least control how you respond to it.

I will quickly add here that this process of forgiveness should never prevent you from reporting abuse or negligence to legal authorities. In fact, it may be the impetus to objectively understand the facts of the matter prior to reporting the offender. Though you may have forgiven your abuser, there still may be a broader social obligation to break your silence and protect others, both in your family and society.

Let's do some more tapping.

Tapping Script 35

KC   Even though I have struggled to forgive [abuser's name], I love and accept who I am.

KC   Even though I have been unable to forgive [abuser's name], I love and forgive myself.

KC   Even though I am only now seeing [abuser's name] as he or she really is, I love and forgive myself.

I See You

EB   [Abuser's name].

SE   We share the pain.

UE   Pain upon pain upon pain.

UN   Pain from your [ancestor].

CH   All this pain.

CB   And so on, generation after generation after generation.

UA   Pain upon pain upon pain.

TH   Down the line.

EB   All this abuse.

SE   Down the line.

UE   All this abandonment.

UN   Down the line.

CH   We need to change this.

CB   You and I.

UA   It is time to end this.

TH   For ourselves.

EB   And for us.

SE   For our sake.

UE	For our children's sake.
UN	I say to you now.
CH	I forgive you.
CB	I forgive you.
UA	I forgive you.
TH	Go in peace.

Repeat this script. Let it land and find a new place within your spirit. It's enough to stop here for a while and rest. It's okay to do so. You have done enough.

For those of you who may be in the same struggle with your father and mother as I am, try the following script. Adapt it according to your requirements.

Tapping Script 36

KC	Even though I feel trapped in my family's story, I love and accept who I am.
KC	Even though I struggle with the idea that my father and mother were also wounded in their childhood, I love and forgive myself.
KC	Even though some part of me is protesting the need to forgive my father and mother, I'm just honoring this.

EB   All this anger.

SE   All this fear.

UE   All this stress.

UN   I had to protect myself.

CH   He or she should have tried harder.

CB   What was done feels unforgivable.

UA   But it's time to try.

TH   Can I really move on from this trauma?

EB   They still stand accused.

SE   That will never change.

UE   I'm just naming it now.

UN   I need to reassure my inner child he or she will be safe.

CH   I need help to do this now.

CB   Before I begin.

UA   Why me? Why then?

TH   My mind needs facts.

EB   I need facts.

SE   But there will be more questions than answers.

UE   And I need to move on.

UN	Life's too short.
CH	I need to move on.
CB	Within them is a child.
UA	And he or she needs compassion too.
TH	I can honor the child even if I cannot honor the man or woman.

EB	Yes, this is a safe place to start.
SE	This is something I can do.
UE	I *see* the hardship of your life.
UN	I *see* how vulnerable you were.
CH	The child within can be honored.
CB	I can forgive.
UA	Child to child.
TH	This I can do.

When we move beyond the wounds of our parents, we begin to liberate and create different pathways of communication from our subconscious into our conscious mind. We, in a sense, become our own parent, calming our own inner child so that he or she is no longer subject to the toxic dictates of our personal and ancestral abuses.

Even though I hold little hope that I will ever have any semblance of a truly trusting loving relationship with my parents, I can now accept that it was neither in their power nor in their upbringing to create these circumstances for me or my siblings.

So,

It will begin for me and for all the generations to come. I know this now. My life will become a testament to change. I will bring about an end to the resentment and abandonment that has held sway over my life. So much so, that I will now make this solemn declaration to myself and to the generations of Stryders to come: "Enough is enough!"

I now want to take you to another place, one that you may have never understood or may have rejected long ago. Prayers of forgiveness can have a subtle creative energy that moves us into a place beyond our normal state of being, gently shifting our perceptions in ways that we may not yet fully understand. They can be used not just in any traditional religious sense of the word, but as a means of cultivating an openness to something beyond ourselves.

At times, it can feel quite arduous, even pointless to pray. Yet by setting each heartfelt prayer in motion, it becomes like being a patient miner slowly chipping away in the dark until, suddenly, we hit upon some hidden gold that allows us to experience forgiveness.

In these moments, we can have great shifts in our perception, gifting us with wisdom, knowledge, and new ideas. Part of the process can begin with simply submitting to the fact that some things are just out of our control.

The action of prayer can be a very dynamic one, where we either clarify our own thinking or surrender to forces greater than ourselves, depending upon our spiritual outlook. Remember a prayer, especially a prayer of forgiveness, can ask a lot from you since you are moving to a state of being that requires you to become a forgiver—no easy task.

One of the prayers that I use to build my own muscle of forgiveness is the Hawaiian, Ho'Oponopono prayer. It is a short and powerful prayer that you can listen to on YouTube. It is also regarded as the "cleaning meditation."

The prayer is as follows:

I love you.

I'm sorry.

Please forgive me.

Thank you.

Dr. Hew Len, who teaches about the use of this prayer, explains that we are all interconnected and that we each mirror the other's wounds. So, effectively, using this prayer is a way to clean out *all* our shared iniquities and vices together. In this way, the healing intention is universal and unconditional.

So keep saying this beautiful, simple prayer over and over again, until it starts to really land with you. Try it at different times of the day, in different situations, as well as in different states of mind. I, myself, often listen to it while doing some knitting, just so that it sinks deeper into my subconscious.

Prayer adds another strategy to our psychological skill set, strengthening our adult mind so that we can undertake a meaningful conversation about forgiveness.

Exercise

Play the "Ho'oponopono: Healing Meditation.

Use the prayer and imagine yourself hearing from an immediate or extended family member who abused or abandoned you. Receive it as the apology you have always wanted and deserved. Spend as much time as you need accepting this prayer of forgiveness.

Feel the inner barricades of your heart breaking down, washed away in waves of newfound relief and grace. As always, go easy on yourself. Be reminded that this is a safe and private space of ritual and healing.

Breathe and focus upon the depth and quality of these exchanges and the relief you are hopefully experiencing. Light a candle to honor your family line, directing your final prayers to all their inner children.

I sincerely hope that you have found these techniques useful. I know that, for many, it has been a powerful yet gentle way of reaching those places of healing once denied to them.

Finally, with all kindness and humility, I invite you to move toward a place of forgiveness. This may be physically impossible to do since the person may have passed away, or you are not yet ready to fully let go.

Even considering letting go of whatever resentment and anger you possess is already enough. Never forget that this is a huge conscious effort that you are undertaking. It may be something that has been present in your ancestral line for centuries.

As I mentioned, we all remain works in progress to our dying day. So at least try to see the possibilities of this, try to understand that we are all capable of overcoming our own personal past and history. In this way, we can move beyond our pain, beyond our anger, beyond our resentment and, most importantly, beyond our abuse.

So, dear reader, let love in.

Ritual

Light a candle for your inner child. And say to him or her,

I give thanks to the possibilities,

the insights,

and the peace,

I have gained so far.

But I will always remember.

It is you my dear child,

I do this for.

It is you who must be protected.

It is you who has borne so much,

On your own,

And at great cost.

I will never allow you to be hurt like that again.

Let me now carry the burden,

Let me now do the work,

Let me now create forgiveness.

For us.

For now.

For always.

Blessed be.

EPILOGUE

AND SO THERE you have it, my journey out of abuse. At each stage, I have tried to share with you my legacy and my destiny, which began long before I was born and still may continue after I am gone.

I can say now, I am part of the solution and not the problem. I have found the means and the opportunities to end the effects of abuse that have been part of my life for so long. And for that, I am truly, truly grateful.

I ask now that you continue your journey back to your heartland, back to that which is most sacred to you—a place you may know exists but have yet to reach. You have once been discarded and abandoned, it is your time now to reclaim your dignity and value.

I have genuine faith that I have given you a seat at the table, the start of a conversation that must continue if we are to achieve real joy in this world. For this reason, I have dedicated the book to all our inner children, in the hope that one day the sweet peace of healing and forgiveness will touch us all.

So love your inner child. Let them know they have come home to you, and it is safe to come out to play.

I see you.

Brigit x

Lightning Source UK Ltd.
Milton Keynes UK
UKHW041123281222
414292UK00021B/9